# COLOUR
# CODING
## for Learners with Autism

A Resource for Creating Meaning through
Colour at Home and School

Adele Devine

Illustrated by Quentin Devine

Jessica Kingsley *Publishers*
London and Philadelphia

All photographs have been reproduced with kind permission
from the parents of the children featured in them.
Figure 3.6 is reproduced with kind permission from Duje Tandin.
Figure 4.4 is reproduced with kind permission from www.tinknstink.co.uk.
Figure 6.7 is reproduced with kind permission from www.do2learn.com.
Figure 8.1 is reproduced from the 'Colourful Semantics' App
with kind permission from London SLTS Ltd.
Figures 8.2, 8.7 and 8.8 are reproduced with kind permission from Learning Resources.
Figure 9.7 is reproduced with kind permission from Joseph Joseph.
Figure 9.8 is reproduced with kind permission from Rainbow Colours.
Figure 10.8 is reproduced with kind permission from New Struan School.
Figure 15.1 is reproduced with kind permission from Paul Isaacs.
Figure 16.1 is reproduced with kind permission from Luna Lindsey.

First published in 2014
by Jessica Kingsley Publishers
73 Collier Street
London N1 9BE, UK
and
400 Market Street, Suite 400
Philadelphia, PA 19106, USA

*www.jkp.com*

**Library of Congress Cataloging in Publication Data**
Devine, Adele.
 Colour coding for learners with autism : a practical resource book / Adele Devine ; illustrated by
Quentin Devine.
     pages cm
 Includes bibliographical references and index.
 ISBN 978-1-84905-441-6 (alk. paper)
 1. Autistic children--Education. 2. Autistic youth--Education. 3. Color--Therapeutic use. 4. Teaching--
Aids and devices. 5. Synaesthesia. I. Title. II. Title: Color coding for learners with autism.
 LC4717.5.D48 2014
 371.9--dc23
                                            2013034390

**British Library Cataloguing in Publication Data**
A CIP catalogue record for this book is available from the British Library

ISBN 978 1 84905 441 6
eISBN 978 0 85700 812 1

Printed and bound in China

For those who love rainbows
more than pots of gold

# ACKNOWLEDGEMENTS

My first and biggest thank you has to be to Quentin because without him all this would be just an idea. He has lovingly created every symbol, schedule and resource. He is also the most supportive husband and an amazing dad to our three children, Malachy, Donovan and Darcy.

It's impossible to express what we both owe to my amazing parents for their unconditional love, constant encouragement and belief. I thank them for teaching me to go ahead and create my own path.

A special thank you to my cousin, Louise Bulmer, who lived in the house next door to me when I was a child. Louise is non-verbal and has been severely physically disabled by cerebral palsy since birth. Without the use of spoken words or body language Louise communicates through facial expressions and sounds. I learnt to read her eyes and draw on instinct to find meanings which enabled us to communicate. She has a brilliant mind, an incredible sense of humour and more spirit than anyone else I know. Louise taught me to cross communication channels and focus on the 'can do' possibilities.

Thank you to all the children, parents and teachers I have had the honour to work with. They have been the best, most colourful teacher teachers.

Thank you, also, to those adults with autism and parents on the autism 'journey' who have shared their individual experiences through books, blogs and forums. Your writing constantly refreshes and inspires.

Finally, a massive thank you to everyone at Jessica Kingsley Publishers for the enthusiasm they have shown for this project from the very start.

# CONTENTS

# LIST OF PRINTABLE RESOURCES

The resources on the CD-ROM can be printed and mounted on card or laminated. There is an extensive set of symbols organised by colour categories. An appropriately coloured CD icon has been added beneath the figures in the book that show visuals of symbols or worksheets found on the CD-ROM. It is our hope that the tailored resources on the CD-ROM at the back of this book will help sort out some of the visual clutter, thereby creating order and help with generalisation. Giving the child with autism clear directions should encourage them to stay on the education 'train'.

### Timetable and timers
Timetable size, 'arrow' symbols
Timetable size, square symbols
Token size, 'arrow' symbols
Token size, square symbols
Purple backing
Purple transition board
Short schedules
Coloured egg timers
Time tracker timer symbols
Whoops symbols
Carousel symbols

### Social and emotional
Social circles
'I can' resources
Volume control resource
Half-sized volume control resource

### Personal care
Timetable size, 'vest' symbols
Timetable size, square symbols
Token size, 'vest' symbols

Token size, square symbols
Washing line schedule
Token board (3 symbols)
Token board (5 symbols)
Bathroom schedules
Cutting nails schedules
Dressing/undressing schedules
Bedtime schedule
Aqua backing

### Sport
Timetable size, 'circle' symbols
Timetable size, square symbols
Token size, 'circle' symbols
Token size, square symbols
Sports token board (3 symbols)
Sports token board (5 symbols)
Sports schedule
'I can' resources

### Colour-coded symbols
More, finished, help, toilet symbols
4 'good' symbols
Toilet transition board
Toilet token board (3 symbols)
Toilet token board (5 symbols)
Toilet symbols

### Food
Food 'bread roll' symbols
Food square symbols
Token board (3 symbols)
Token board (5 symbols)
Blank 'bread roll' symbols
I want/would like boards

### Behaviour

Timetable size, 'thumbs up' symbols

Timetable size, square symbols

Token size, 'thumbs up' symbols

Token size, square symbols

Token board (3 symbols)

Token board (5 symbols)

### Traffic lights and volume control

Traffic lights resource

Half-sized traffic lights resource

Volume control resource

Half-sized volume control resource

Asking for help resource

Half-sized asking for help resource

Bag tags resource

### Teaching true colours and floor spots

Colour symbols

Colour symbols small

I see resources

Colour umbrella resources

'I can' resources

8 floor spots (shapes)

8 shapes, small

8 floor spots (circles)

8 circles, small

# PREFACE

'Do not train a child to learn by force or harshness; but direct them to it by what amuses their minds, so that you may be better able to discover with accuracy the peculiar bent of the genius of each.'

Plato

## Camp Eagle Springs, Pennsylvania, USA; summer of '99

Bill kept his bald head down. He avoided attention, never speaking or making eye contact. He followed along, always on the outside, doing just enough to comply. Bill would spend hours creating patchwork pictures with wax crayons. His artwork consisted of bright, strong patches of colour with no gaps or overlaps. It was simple, intense, unique and beautiful.

'I really like the colour of the sky – such an amazing blue,' I said dreamily, more to myself than to Bill. He paused, then put down the crayon he was using. When he lifted a light blue crayon, I felt like dancing. Bill started to colour again. After a few moments, sensing the blue patch was almost complete, I mentioned how the colour of fresh green grass made me feel happy. The blue crayon went back in the pot and he started to colour with a grassy green. Each time I said something positive about a colour, Bill changed crayons. There was a huge selection of colours and he always selected the shade to match my description. Bill never looked up, but there was a shift in atmosphere. We were communicating within his comfort zone.

I tested further, 'I don't like bright orange at all. It hurts my eyes.' Bill paused. He did not change colour. After a while he continued with the crayon he had. We carried on like this – a colourful version of the game 'Simon Says'.

Bill seemed so withdrawn and hard to reach, but we made a connection through those coloured crayons. When he finished his picture, I praised him. His eyes revealed a flicker of recognition – perhaps the hint of an inner smile?

Camp Eagle Springs was a magical place. I worked as a camp counsellor, spending three amazing months caring for adults with learning difficulties. I found I was totally at home with adults with autism and loved being in their company. There was the man who would run without warning, and the one who pulled my hair so many times that I wore a wig. Then there were the savants with such amazing abilities… I remember one man who could tear paper into any picture. He kept all his pictures in a pile and carried them everywhere. If asked to find the picture of an apple, he could locate it right away from the pile. Another man could recall details of every band that had been in the charts, and there was someone else who made a point of knowing everyone's birthday. There was the man who would pop all the balloons and the one who threw me across the noisy barn, then five minutes later we were playing 'pattercake' as though nothing had happened.

Then there were the quieter ones, like Bill, who preferred to disappear into their own world and tap a cup. There was something so exhilarating about seeking the hidden keys and making connections. These adults were a beautiful puzzle. I loved everything about them.

My sensory-seeking adults would often end up at the art barn, aware that it was the place to find touchy-feely clay and paints. There was also the pull of finding shade from the summer sun. Quentin was the clay tutor on camp. I noticed how he tuned in to what motivated each and every individual and helped them believe in themselves. I remember one lesson when Quentin was making egg cups and one of the adults (my runner) was showing no interest. 'John really loves his mum,' I hinted, and Quentin immediately took the prompt. He coaxed John into making an egg cup for his mum. Quentin was forever patient, always smiling, and would take time to tune in to complex individuals, engaging them to try by using whatever they loved. He understood and enjoyed their quirks. As I grew to love the adults in my care, I also fell completely in love with their best teacher.

Mini-breakthroughs and being 'let in' felt magical because many of these adults had been 'stuck' for years. A lot of them spent the rest of the year in institutions. I wondered how much time they usually spent rocking, flicking and zoning out.

## Special education

I loved working with those adults, but wished I could have met them as children and before they had the chance to get so 'stuck'. I could see their intelligence, their truth and humour and knew instinctively that their lives could have been different.

I knew then that I wanted to work with children with autism and to ensure that 'can do' discoveries were made early on. These adults had deserved a better chance. I owed it to them to find a way to change outcomes, open doors and empower future children with autism to fulfil their potential. After camp I found an amazing job – home-tutoring children on the Applied Behaviour Analysis (ABA) programme. I worked with two incredible boys and their families. One boy loved traffic lights so much he used to sleep with a toy one. The other boy did not speak, but would communicate by typing on a laptop. They taught me so much and made me realise I was a teacher.

Five years later, Quentin and I were married. I was teaching at a school for children with severe learning difficulties and autism. Quentin was working as a web designer. In the evenings after work he would create animations to engage my individual learners. 'If you could put a T-rex beside Chloe's name and make it roar, I'm certain she could learn to spell her name', I'd say. Seeing how these activities motivated the children inspired us to create our award-winning SEN Assist software (another story).

## Why colour coding?

I then spent many happy years teaching at an autism-specific school, learning strategies and gaining insights into how these children learn. I was always looking for ways to improve things. I knew the provision was excellent and all the most up-to-the-minute strategies were being used, but I was convinced that things could be better. I noticed that we were using colour codes everywhere. We were using colours to clarify tasks, sort visual clutter and motivate. I began to research the relationship between individuals with autism and colours, and found connection after connection. Walk into any school and see how colour is used to create structure, explain, sort and guide. Purpose-built autism-specific schools now incorporate colour into their architecture to help create a more productive and happy learning environment.

Colour is so often used in our everyday lives. Imagine negotiating the underground lines in London without the colour-coded tube maps. Think of traffic lights, stamps and most board games.

People with autism are so often visual learners, and colours are much quicker to decode than language. Science is revealing that autistic children may see faster than other children. Research using eye-tracking technology has shown that autistic children are more drawn to looking at colours and shapes than their typically developing peers.

I've also found clues from history. Many famous talented people from our past who have been posthumously diagnosed as having autism are documented as having been fascinated by light and colour. Isaac Newton had an early obsession with sundials and came up with the Theory of Colour before discovering gravity. Many of the great artists, musicians, writers, scientists and inventors seem to have autism-related traits to their characters. Think of Einstein, Mozart, Van Gogh… Are we allowing individuals to develop their talents with our current teaching methods? Is there more or maybe less we should be doing?

## Creating a practical resource

Is there a way of taking what we already understand and do to support people with autism further? Could we exploit colour coding to teach people with autism to map concepts, generalise ideas, store their learning and even increase their independence? Could we tap in on what adults with autism have told us about how they think, and use it to develop new strategies and supports? Could there be a way of using the shapes and colours that children with autism naturally tune in to in order to help them decode more ambiguous things, such as social interactions? I looked at the visuals we were using in school and found that they were not perfect. I knew that if we got the visuals right we would be closer to helping these children decode situations. We would require a host of new resources and this would require another type of thinker. I needed an artist, a designer, and because I had no budget it would have to be someone who wholeheartedly believed in my ideas.

At the back of the book there is a CD-ROM packed with colour-coded symbols, worksheets and practical resources. Images have been specifically created to illustrate, explain and decode, like a social underground map. The symbols have not only been colour coded, but each one has been freshly designed to make sense and appeal to the literal learner. Quentin has transformed my teacher ideas into practical resources. Each resource is made with the love and attention to detail that children with autism crave. The figures in this book show how the resources can be used in practice.

This book is not *just* a new theory about how we can use colour to help learners with autism, but also a practical teaching tool.

I've spent so many years involved in autism education that I've tuned in to how these children learn. The visuals on the resource CD-ROM were designed to improve the child's journey in the same way that perfect road signs help a driver. The more clearly we can show children what we want, the more chance they have of getting things right.

This is a practical resource book for anyone involved in educating young people with autism. My aim is to sort the jumble of information we throw at these children and present it in such a way that they will have a greater chance of achieving future independence and fulfilment.

## A note on vocabulary

For ease of reading we have used male pronouns to refer to a hypothetical child and female pronouns to refer to a teacher/support worker.

# Chapter 1
# True Colours

'The purest and most thoughtful minds are
those which love colour the most.'

John Ruskin

Colours are companions to children with autism. Amidst so many threatening things that bombard them on a daily basis, their colours provide a point of contact. Colours are familiar and beautiful. Before we begin to teach children our colour labels, they may have linked their colours to numerous ideas and functions, categorising them by their multiple hues and subtle variations.

Long before these children learn language, they may have learnt to use colours to bring order to chaos – to decode the world. So when we start to use colour labels, we must take care that we do not confuse or contradict what the child with autism already *knows*.

Imagine if your best friend suddenly changes her name. She no longer wants to be called 'Sarah Jane'. From now on she wants to be known as 'Jenny'. If you had never met her before and she told you her name was 'Jenny', that would be okay, but she is expecting you to unlearn the name you have always known. You accidentally call her 'Sarah Jane'. She corrects you. Her tone is slightly patronising. How would you feel?

We must take care about how we introduce our colour labels to children with autism. We teach them that the lemon is 'yellow', but then apply the same colour label to a pepper that is a 'different' colour 'yellow'. The lemon and the pepper are both cold food. Does that mean yellow is the word for cold food? Next time we show them a 'yellow' duck.

*Figure 1.1 A 'yellow' lemon and a 'yellow' pepper (the colours are not the same)*

The yellows are *not* the same, so how can they have the same label? This may contradict how a visual learner thinks of colours. Imagine if you were told that from now on pens, pencils, chalks and crayons would not have separate labels. To make things simple they would all be referred to as 'writes'. Would this seem easier or more confusing? Learners with autism are known for their attention to detail. They relentlessly pursue the truth. We must always keep this in mind.

The colour-matching worksheet portrayed in Figure 1.2 could really confuse visual learners. They might see the individual colours in so much detail. How can they match the 'same' colour. The colours and labels are not the same. They may not categorise two different yellows together or generalise in this way and we must not assume they will.

We may have thought that colour language is one of the first types of vocabulary children learn. The earliest toys we give our children often have a colour-based theme. For example, baby toys speak the colour when the child presses the button. The concept seems basic, but is it?

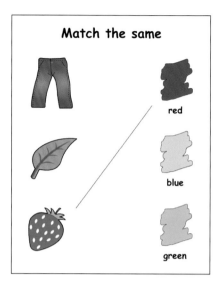

*Figure 1.2 A colour-matching worksheet (this could confuse visual learners)*

Jeanne Brohart shares her experience of teaching colours to her son Zachary:

> Zachary had a very difficult time learning colours…at least in expressing them to me. I worked and worked with him on that…but, for the longest time, no matter what I did, Zachary just didn't seem to 'get it'… So I thought!
>
> I couldn't understand why something that seemed like such an 'easy thing' was so difficult to teach… After all…red was red, blue was blue, green was green, etc. What was so hard about that? Given what I now believe to understand about the importance and role of colours in the life of the autistic child, it is my opinion that the concept of 'colours' was difficult for Zachary to grasp because he himself had been making use of this concept as a coping mechanism…to make sense of his own world.

She goes on to explain that, looking back, she believes it would have been better to introduce one colour at a time when teaching a child with autism:

> If I had to do this over again, I'd start with just one colour. For example, I'd cover 'blue', 'navy blue', 'royal blue', etc., before moving on to the next colour. The autistic mind is so accurate and so precise in its thinking, that I suspect Zachary may have 'coded' hues of colours himself…and if I then introduced these 'hues' of blue as something different than what he knew them to be in his own 'coding system', then I was potentially

introducing an unknown…potentially interfering with 'his code' and 'his understanding of the world based on that code'. (Brohart 2002)

Research shows that children find it difficult to learn colour words and are much quicker to learn the names of objects. Researchers at the University of Nottingham, UK, and McGill University, Canada, tried to find out why toddlers find colour words difficult to learn. They asked the question, 'Is there something special about colour that prevents toddlers learning colour words easily?' They conducted tests and found that children saw differences between colours in the first few months of life. They could tell different colours apart before knowing the names. Colours grabbed their attention. The toddlers would often use colour to group objects. They could see and use colour, but would confuse colour words (Pitchford and Mullen 2002).

Children with autism may really know their colours and be able to use them, but translating this to language takes much longer. When teaching children with autism, should we hold off expecting them to use colour labels for a longer time than we do with those who are developing typically? Labelling colours causes problems for toddlers who have acquired an extensive vocabulary of objects and verbs. So are we being unfair in expecting a pre-verbal child with autism to label colours before he has caught up with all the other words? (Pitchford and Mullen found that the toddlers learnt to recognise colours long before they could successfully name them.)

Children with autism may seek comfort in their colours. Daniel Tammet was diagnosed with Asperger's Syndrome by Professor Simon Baron-Cohen. He came into the spotlight when he gained the European record for reciting pi from memory to 22,514 digits in five hours and nine minutes on 14 March 2004. Tammet's unique mind enables him to learn a new language in a week and solve the most complex mathematical equations in his head. He recalls in his memoir *Born on a Blue Day* the early 'obsession' he had with the colourful 'Mr Men' books: 'I spent hours in the evenings lying on the floor with the books in my hands, looking at the colours and shapes in the illustrations… For the first time I seemed happy and peaceful' (Tammet 2007, p.29).

We are lucky now to have access to so many books and blogs written by adults with autism. They provide us with a valuable window, allowing us to see how the child with autism might see. Reading their memoirs I've found what I believe is a common thread running through each individual story – an early love affair with colours.

Children with autism feel comfortable and secure with their colours. They spend as much time as they can with them. I believe that children with autism don't just like colours, they love them intensely. They know them individually. They may in time find a new love, but the colours retain a hold on their hearts as do all first loves.

We refer to those we love using their individual name or a pet name. When we teach children with autism to name the colours, we must tread carefully. We cannot afford to get something so important wrong.

Kristine Barnett, author of *The Spark. A Mother's Story of Nurturing Genius*, recalls how at two-and-a-half her autistic son Jake created a beautiful rainbow on the floor using a multitude of coloured crayons. She was stunned to realise that they were in the correct order of the spectrum. She recalls the conversation she had the next morning at the breakfast table with her husband Michael.

> 'How can he possibly know the order of the colour spectrum?' I asked. 'I could barely remember ROYGBIV!' As if in response, Jake reached out to the table and turned the faceted water glass in front of Michael so it caught the morning sunshine pouring in from the sliding door, splashing a gorgeous, full-spectrum rainbow across the kitchen floor. 'I guess that's how he knows,' Michael said. (Barnett 2013a, p.42)

Shortly after Jake turned four, she reflects on how he had 'become interested in examining light and colours chemically'. He found observing the colourful signatures of gases 'as profoundly moving and emotionally intense as an architecture buff seeing the cathedral at Chartres, or a lover of Impressionist art left alone in a room lined with Monet's water lilies' (Barnett 2013b, p.95).

Isaac Newton (posthumously diagnosed with autism) took finding the truth about colours to an extreme by poking pointed sticks behind his eye sockets. Wiggling the stick back as far as it would go caused him to see coloured circles. He wanted to know where the colour came from. He also spent hours staring at the sun, almost blinding himself, and had to spend days recovering.

Newton's next step was using a prism. He allowed a thin ray of sunlight through the curtain to hit the prism and projected a spectrum of colours on the wall. He realised that white light is not pure at all, but made up of all the colours of the rainbow. No one would understand the reasons behind Newton's strange behaviour until much later in his life.

## How do children first learn colours?

Melody Dye and Professor Michael Ramscar spent several years studying how children learn language, particularly the colour words. They conducted a series of simple colour recognition tests on a number of two-year-olds to see if they could name the basic colours. The majority of the toddlers failed to label the colours correctly.

Dye and Ramscar investigated why learning colours took children so long. They found that the number of colour hues could be one cause of the difficulties. They suggested that variants in culture and language were also factors. The way we use colour language is not universal or consistent.

> What all this means is that the learning problem exists in not only learning a word to color mapping, but also in learning the peculiar color 'maps' your language uses in the first place. The task is further complicated by the fact that color is ubiquitous in everyday life. At any given time, we are surrounded by a multitude of hues, as we move through a world of faces and places, objects and surroundings. This overwhelming ubiquity is not a feature of other common words, such as nouns. (Dye 2011, p.51)

Dye and Ramscar found that children learnt colour words faster if they introduced them as they would a proper noun. Rather than labelling 'the red balloon', they would describe it as 'the balloon that is red'.

When introducing colour words to children with autism, we need to show that colour words are like blankets that can be used to label many shades and variants. By calling 'navy blue' just 'blue' we are not 'lying' or 'misrepresenting', but simplifying. Not easy to grasp for the specific, detail-conscious, literal learner. However, there are visual ways to help.

I looked at the symbols we are currently using for pre-verbal children to label colours. I suddenly saw how they could confuse a literal learner.

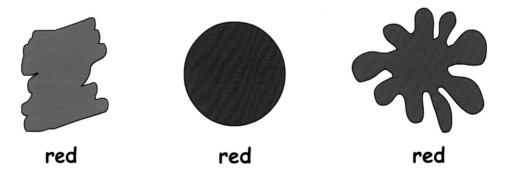

*Figure 1.3 Three different red symbols*

Joseph Albers said:

> If one says 'Red' (the name of a colour) and there are 50 people listening, it can be expected that there will be 50 reds in their minds. And one can be sure that all these reds will be very different colours. (Albers 1975, p.3)

Which of the symbols in Figure 1.4 says 'blue' as we would expect it to be used in everyday speech? The multi-tone symbol might seem more complex, but to the literal, visual learner it communicates more effectively that we are using the word 'blue' as a blanket term. Children with autism are often said to find it difficult to generalise. Could the multi-tone blue symbol be a stepping stone towards using language in a more general way?

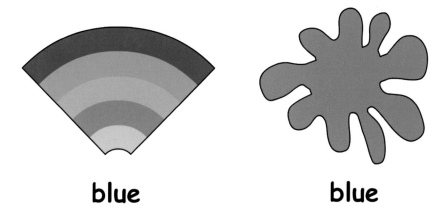

blue        blue

*Figure 1.4 Two different blue symbols*

Our visuals must account for the learner's attention to detail in order to avoid confusion. The autistic artist and author Judy Endow explains that for her 'Each color, with its infinite variety of hues and brightness, has its own movement patterns and sound combinations' (Endow 2009).

Author Luna Lindsey reflects on her personal experience of having Asperger's in her blog. When it comes to describing colours she has to be accurate. She explains:

> I have a keen sense of honesty. To a fault, sometimes. If I'm making a statement, I feel the need to qualify it to ensure I am telling the complete truth. I cannot simply say, 'The sky is blue', because if there is a cloud in it, it's technically a bit white, and I feel I am lying if I don't qualify. (Lindsey 2013)

If you are used to set colour symbols, the sight of new ones may raise your heckles, but I believe they illustrate that the colour words are blanket labels.

Think how rigid some children can be, always wanting the same snack, the same seat or the same route to the park. We cannot afford to introduce concepts in the wrong way, because unlearning can be much harder than learning.

Why not try teaching colour labels in a way that worked for Dye and Ramscar? This might make more sense to visual learners. Print the colour matching resources from the resource CD-ROM. Point to the items and use the less natural way to label them, as suggested by Melody Dye: 'The duck that is yellow', 'The cup that is blue.' If Dye and Ramscar found this helped their two-year-old verbal study group to develop language faster, then let's see if their shortcut helps learners with autism (Dye 2011).

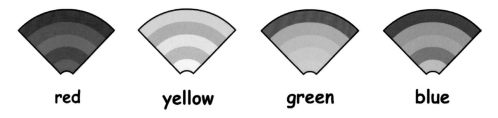

red            yellow            green            blue

*Figure 1.5 Four true colour symbols*

Explore colours one at a time in a patient, kind and respectful way. Nurture their relationship, exploring the subtle variations and shades of each individual colour. Let the children see that you share their love of colours. Mirror the way they explore, and share in their wonder.

Blow bubbles – all children love them. They are visual, calming and colourful. They will get the child's interest. Daniel Tammet recalls how, when a nursery assistant blew bubbles, he 'loved the way the light reflected off their shiny, wet surface' (Tammet 2007, p.27). When someone is blowing bubbles, they do not use lots of confusing language and they create something beautiful. This will appeal to the visual learner and provide a point of contact.

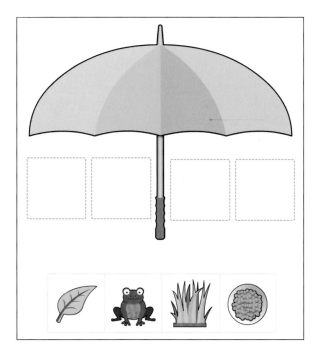

*Figure 1.6 A coloured umbrella resource*

Children may take steps back if we present something that they view as confusing or contradictory. When teaching children with autism it is vital that we build trust and that they are confident in our ability as teachers. They must be able to look to us for the right answers. They *know* their colours, but do we?

## Ideas for teaching the individual colours

There are so many ways to explore colour, beyond using worksheets.

- Painting exploration boxes in different colours and then filling them with random objects of those colours is a great way to explore and name different shades. The boxes containing A4 paper sent to the school office make great colour collection boxes.

- You can also add food dye and scents to rice, pasta, shaving foam, cornflower and water, washing-up liquid or playdough.

### Green

*Art*: Let the children create their own trees by doing leaf rubbings with green crayons.

*Sensory*: Make lime jelly and put it in sensory trays with sliced frozen limes.

*Outing*: Enjoy a nature hunt in an evergreen forest. Give each child a collection basket to collect as many greens as possible.

### Red

*Art*: Look at poppy fields. Create a poppy display by sticking red tissue onto poppy templates, then cut them out and use them to cover a green field background.

*Sensory*: Make rose-scented, red playdough and give it to the children when it is still warm. Show them how to make mini playdough cupcakes in red silicone cases. Decorate with red beads or buttons and put them on a baking tray. You could even make a red-hot oven out of cardboard for them.

*Outing*: Post a red letter in a red postbox. Maybe make and post a Valentine's card?

### Blue

*Art*: Create an under-the-sea collage with paint swirls. Pour different blue paints into a tray and let the children swirl them around and mix them either with their hands or using a paintbrush. Place a piece of paper onto the paint to print their 'art'. Create the fish and other sea creatures by using simple templates. Cut out tiny squares of blue tissue, plastic bags and sweet wrappers, then get the children to create fish collages.

*Sensory*: Add blue food dye to the water tray with blue ice, boats, plastic polar bears and penguins.

*Outing*: Visit a garden centre, pet shop or Sea Life Centre to see fish in the aquariums.

## Yellow

*Art*: Cut lemons in half, dip them in yellow paint and use them to print yellow buttercups.

*Sensory*: Make a large quantity of lemon jelly and put it in transparent sensory tubs with sliced frozen lemons. Put a lid on to seal the tubs, then explore by shining a torch and looking at the light shining through the jelly. This is really effective in a dark room or tent.

*Outing*: Visit the supermarket with a shopping list of yellow items to buy – bananas, lemons, yellow washing-up gloves.

# Ideas for sorting colours

There are so many ways to sort by colour:

- Paint charts can be a good way to show variations of colour. Matching activities made from paint colour charts can also reveal an impressive ability to distinguish and group colours.

- Why not collect coloured bottle tops and have the children sort them into coloured bowls or post them as coins into coloured containers?

- Make coloured postboxes and have children sort the post by colour.

- Paint cardboard tubes, secure them to the side of a table and have the children drop coloured pom-poms down the correct colour tube. Have a coloured bucket at the bottom to collect them.

- Put pretend matchsticks into coloured matchboxes.

- Decorate playdough buns with buttons in muffin trays.

- Thread coloured beads onto pipe cleaners with a corresponding colour.

- Scour the internet for inspiration and ideas. There are so many things you can do…

Once a child is confident with colour labels, we can introduce the way that colour words are most often used in everyday speech. We can ask, 'What do you see?' and clearly model the sentence structure that is more frequently used. For example, 'I see a red strawberry.' You could add a bold line around the object so that the child makes the visual link and knows where to place the symbols. Or you could use a colour that links with colourful semantics (see Chapter 8 for more information).

*Figure 1.7 I see resource*

How early can children make colour connections? I was pleased when at the age of three our son announced, 'My favourite colour is red.' He stuck to it. He had a red scooter, a red bike and a red coat. Great, I thought – an original mind. He has not fallen for the whole 'blue for boys' thing.

About a year later we were walking back from pre-school, when he suddenly announced, 'My favourite colour is blue.'

'But you like red. You've always said red is your favourite colour?' I said, hoping he would stick to his guns.

'No, I don't like red now. I like blue.' For a moment my heart sunk. Was he following the crowd? Had he made a connection that boys like blue? (Toy shops encourage us to buy blue for boys and pink for girls.)

I am all for original choice, but, if he had chosen pink instead of red, my protective instinct would be to somehow override his originality. I would not feel comfortable sending him to school with a pink lunchbox in case some other child made it an issue.

Are boys and girls naturally drawn to blue and pink or are they programmed by toys in those colours to gravitate towards them?

Researchers at the University of Cambridge conducted a study to find out if boys and girls showed a natural preference for certain colours. The study involved 120 children aged 12, 18 and 24 months. They concluded that 'There were no significant sex differences in infants' preferences for different colours or shapes. Instead, both girls and boys preferred reddish colours over blue and rounded over angular shapes' (Jadva, Hines and Golombok 2010, p.2).

At four, favourite colours *are* important. Friendships can be based on having the same favourite colour. When our second son started school, each child was asked to put their name on a piece of coloured paper. He went straight to blue. I was relieved that the teacher had allowed the children to choose their colour. She later based her class organisation around those groups. If she had not given the children choice and had selected the wrong colour for our son, this could have had a negative effect. Being in blue group was motivating and made him happy.

As the child explores colours and shapes, be on the lookout for any signs of preference. Is it one colour, one shade or is it seeing colours all together? Never stop looking for the detail in what these children love. Find out what motivates individual children because their motivator is often the key to creating a desire to learn.

# Chapter 2
# Colour-Coded Symbols

'Truth is ever to be found in the simplicity, and not
in the multiplicity and confusion of things.'

Isaac Newton

Imagine you are in an unfamiliar place and need the toilet. You look around, but there is no sign. There are lots of people, but you can't communicate with them because they don't understand your language. This is getting urgent and you're starting to panic. Children with listening and communication difficulties associated with autism face this situation every day and there are some simple ways we can avoid it.

*Figure 2.1 A colour-coded 'toilet' symbol*

Most settings now provide some visual symbol to indicate toilet. Most often it will be black and white. Children need to be taught that this symbol represents toilet and how to use it to communicate their need. They will learn this by repetitive use of the symbol. Each time they go to the toilet they take the symbol and match it to one that is the same in the toilet. Sometimes children need to start off with a photograph of the actual toilet rather than a symbol. Give them a laminated photograph of the toilet and have them take this and match it to a transition board located on the door to the toilet.

If the child wears nappies, make the symbol or photograph a nappy or changing area. Some children might need to use an object of reference and take the actual nappy along. Use whatever works for the individual child.

Donna Williams (an adult author with autism) talks about how people with autism may use the sink, the bath or shower as a toilet because they all have the same ceramic texture and colour. She suggests using colour to distinguish the toilet in a single colour bathroom suite: 'You can paint the toilet a different colour from the rest of the suite so it is clear that it is part of a different category and keep all choices clearly distinguished from one another' (Williams 1996).

If you were to invest in a yellow toilet seat or paint the area around the toilet yellow, it could encourage a visual link. This may sound quite drastic, but compare it to the alternative... As the child learns that the toilet is the place to go, the need for the colour code will be reduced. Dr Temple Grandin is an American doctor of animal science, bestselling author, autistic activist and consultant to the livestock industry on animal behaviour. Grandin was diagnosed with autism at the age of two and did not start to speak until she was four. She explains that:

A common problem is that a child may be able to use the toilet correctly at home but refuses to use it at school. This may be due to a failure to recognise the toilet. Hilde De Clercq from Belgium discovered that an autistic child may use a small non-relevant detail to recognise an object such as a toilet. It takes detective work to find that detail. In one case a boy would only use the toilet at home that had a black seat. His parents and teacher were able to get him to use the toilet at school by covering its white seat with black tape. The tape was then gradually removed and toilets with white seats were now recognised as toilets. (Grandin 2002)

*Figure 2.2 A toilet door with toilet transition board and symbols*

To help children learn to transition, hand them the yellow toilet symbol as shown in Figure 2.1 and guide them to match it to the transition board on the toilet door. Say 'toilet' when you show them the symbol to reinforce and promote understanding of the spoken word. In time the child should learn to transition independently when given the symbol. You could use the smaller colour-coded 'toilet' symbols to create a token system so that each time the children use the toilet they get a symbol on their token board leading to a motivating reward.

*Figure 2.3 A colour-coded 'more' symbol*

Children may need a motivator to begin to communicate. When starting out using Picture Exchange Communication System (PECs), children use a picture to request something that they want. We teach them to take a photograph or symbol and give it to us to request their motivator. This might be food or a favourite toy. Snack time can be a good time to start a child with PECs (if food is a motivator). As soon as the picture is given, the request should be honoured. We build as many exchanges or opportunities for communication into the day as possible.

We may gradually build a bank of photographs, but there will be times when we don't have a photograph or symbol and we don't want to lose the moment. Having a stock of 'more' symbols can be a useful standby – for example, if a child likes bubbles being blown or you find a snack the child likes but you don't have a symbol for these, teach him to ask for 'more' instead. Make sure you say the word each time you use the symbol and quickly introduce the idea of using it for other motivators.

*Figure 2.4 A colour-coded 'help' symbol*

Children with autism are very good at finding ways to get what they want without using speech. Maybe they will take your hand to open the snack cupboard or lead you to open a door so that they can play outside. The 'help' symbol gives them the power to communicate and say, 'I want help'. So, if a child wants to get outside and the door is locked, he can ask even if there is not a handy 'outside' symbol available.

The blue of this symbol may also help children to categorise and generalise 'people who help us' (see Chapter 6 for more details).

Figure 2.5 A colour-coded 'finished' symbol

Hold up this symbol whenever an activity is finished. Use it at the end of a snack, at tidy-up time and at the end of session. Keep it handy by using velcro to stick it under the table, ready to hold up at the end of an activity. Take care not to have a 'finished' symbol out on permanent display or it could send the wrong message. Only symbols which are immediately relevant should be on view.

This symbol can also be used as a postbox for timetable symbols. When an activity is completed, the child posts the symbol behind the 'finished' symbol as shown in Figure 2.6.

Figure 2.6 This red 'finished' symbol is stuck to the wall with velcro at the bottom and sides, and timetable symbols were posted behind it as they finished

As activities are finished, the symbols could also be placed in a red bucket or posted in a red postbox with a red 'finished' symbol attached. The 'finished' symbol also works well on a 'finished work' tray. (Since red is used internationally as the colour for stop signs, it is the only logical choice for a 'finished' symbol.)

You can also use this symbol to request that a challenging behaviour should 'finish' without having to use lots of language. Sometimes language can be seen as rewarding challenging behaviour. Many children use behaviour to get reactions – they don't mind if the reaction is negative. Just as on the football pitch the 'red card' indicates that it is time to stop an unwanted behaviour, so it can be used in the classroom and other situations as a great way to request an unwanted behaviour to stop without reinforcing or adding to the negatives with language.

Be careful how you use the 'finish' symbol though. I once worked very hard to get one of my students to come to our school assemblies. He was at the back and had decided to climb on one of the chairs. Instinctively, I lifted my 'finished' symbol and he happily jumped off the chair and bounced out of the assembly hall. I had meant for the behaviour to finish, *not* the assembly. I did not attempt to explain – we returned to class and our attempts to get him to assembly were back to square one.

## Colour-coded behaviour symbols

The amber colour relates to traffic lights of the 'wait' symbol. The clock on the symbol helps the child to connect waiting with the concept of time, and helps to illustrate that the waiting will not last forever. This symbol was created for children who find waiting difficult. One of the best places to teach this symbol is in the car. Each time you stop at traffic lights or have to wait, show this symbol. When the waiting is over, remove the symbol and praise the child if he has waited calmly.

*Figure 2.7 A colour-coded 'good waiting' symbol*

As a baby, our son would cry when we stopped at traffic lights and then, when we moved on, he would stop crying and look all smug. He thought his noise had made us start moving, so he would do it every time. This is how children learn that their negative behaviour can have an effect on our actions.

I saw the power of this symbol when I arrived at the school ICT room with my class of children with autism and found another class still using it. My expectations were not good and I was anticipating a few meltdowns. But no – they surprised us all. I showed them the 'waiting' symbol and said 'waiting' very calmly and they did just that. This is a powerful symbol.

*Figure 2.8 A colour-coded 'good sitting' symbol*

Sitting still and keeping their hands down is difficult for a lot of children. Many will understand without a visual, but there are those who don't. This symbol shows them exactly what you want them to do. It also means you do not need to keep disrupting the group by telling the child to sit well. However, this symbol is only for use if you are expecting the child to sit in a chair, because children with autism can be very literal.

Individual carpet sample squares can work well to get the children to sit well at carpet time. You can get these for next-to-nothing or even free from carpet shops when you explain their use.

*Figure 2.9 Colour-coded 'good looking' and 'good listening' symbols*

Display 'good sitting', 'good looking' and 'good listening' symbols somewhere prominent, and teach all of the children what they mean. You'll be surprised how quickly they learn them.

Always use symbols to reinforce positive behaviour and show your expectations. Don't have images of negative behaviours, such as 'no throwing' or 'no hitting', because they can easily be misread. If you feel you must display unwanted behaviours, be sure to put a very definite circle and black line through the behaviour rather than have a 'no' symbol next to it. Sometimes a child becomes set on accessing areas that are restricted, for example the school kitchen. A good visual way to show he is not allowed in this area is to display his photograph with a circle around it and a cross through it on the door. When he gets to the door, point to the visual and say, 'No Charlie.' This is sort of visual works well and may be familiar as it is often used on public signs to show restrictions (for example, 'No diving' at the swimming pool). However, I have seen this strategy misinterpreted. A door which has the child's photo next to a 'no' symbol could be viewed as an invitation if the child does not read the 'no'. It's so easy for strategies that start out working well to become lost in translation as they are passed on by teachers. Always look at visuals through fresh eyes, zoom in and assess what they would say if you could not read the words.

The smaller versions of the colour-coded symbols can be used as tokens for token boards. A yellow 'toilet' symbol used as a token gives the child a visual of what each token is for. Attaching visual images to tokens lets the child know what your expectation is. He can make the connection that when he uses the toilet successfully he will get a token. This is less ambiguous than collecting smiley faces or stars.

If you find that any particular symbols or strategies are helping a child, then share them with parents/grandparents – the more consistent their use, the greater their power.

## Why colour code the symbols?

The colour coding of symbols is not a new idea. Some children will connect with the colour before the image. By colour coding the most basic symbols, you include these children and help them to learn that different symbols have different uses.

When you need a symbol fast to suit an immediate need, you quickly learn to find it by colour. Even if children understand black-and-white symbols in calm moments, when they are at crisis point we need to give them the quickest way to communicate their needs. Colour coding the background, as opposed to the actual symbol, is helpful so that the symbol can be seen clearly and provides a visual cue to the user.

Compare children learning colour-coded symbols to how we learn traffic lights. At first we learn to connect red with the word 'stop', but in time we see red and think 'stop'. However, we are not going to teach *every* symbol in this way. In fact, I recommend you limit the colour-filled symbols to the eight shown above.

When working with pre-verbal children with Autistic Spectrum Conditions (ASCs), it is vital that they can access the symbols to communicate basic requests at all times. I recall one little boy who had mastered PECs so well to make requests. It was lunchtime and he had finished his packed lunch, but because other children were still eating I had pointed to the 'good waiting' symbol and requested he do 'good waiting'. This clever little man used the colour-coded symbols and handed me his sentence strip. He pointed to the symbols as I read aloud 'I want good waiting finished please'. He was so bright, so capable of communicating what he wanted in a mature way when the symbols were available. If he could not have told me using his symbols, he may have chosen to use a head-banging tantrum to make his point instead.

If you have already set up a colour-coded system, do not change it. These colour-coded symbols were created as a starting point. If a system is in place that works, the scaffolding is there. Don't take it all down and change it. Clarification is the important thing, not the specific colours used.

## Does having coloured symbols stop children learning to read?

No. When people with autism are experiencing sensory overload or meltdown they may not be able to read symbols. This will not stop them from reading when they are calm and in learning mode. For extreme situations we provide what children can comprehend on their *worst* day. If a red symbol stops them doing something dangerous, does it matter if they read it? If a yellow symbol is the one they grab when they have left it to the last moment to ask for the toilet, would we rather they read or got to the toilet fast? These symbols serve the child in an emergency. The colours are visible from a distance. Support workers and students will learn to use these symbols without reading them. These symbols need to communicate as fast as possible. Of all the symbols we have provided there are only eight that have block colour fill. The images are white with a black outline to ensure they really stand out. If children can learn to use these symbols and start to see that they have a functional purpose they will be off to a great start. Repeatedly use the symbols for 'more', 'finished', 'toilet' and 'help' along with Makaton sign language, and you will be constantly reinforcing functional communication.

## Case study

When Carla started school she had no speech but found other ways to get what she wanted. She could take you by the hand and drag you to where the item she required was kept.

To encourage communication, motivators were either locked in a cupboard or kept out of reach. The aim was that the children would use their symbols or speech to tell us what they wanted. The more they did this the better they got at communicating.

Carla had never used pictures for communication before and was determined that if her usual approach of taking us there was not successful, she would get her motivator (in this case a noisy toy called a 'Sit and Spin').

The 'Sit and Spin' toy was in a cupboard. Carla had seen that we kept the cupboard key high up next to the door frame. This meant the adults could all access the key fast, but the children couldn't.

We watched with admiration as Carla went and got a chair and dragged it to the cupboard then climbed up to reach the key.

We introduced a picture communication system straightaway. We took large photographs of the things she wanted and had some success. We wanted to build the number of exchanges Carla would make during the day, but we could not always predict her request and be armed with a symbol.

Carla had the four colour-coded symbols – More, Finished, Toilet and Help – on the front of her PECs book and we taught her to use them. We would repeatedly model the language that went with the symbols and in time she learnt to use them when the picture she wanted was not available.

With these symbols Carla was able to start communicating her basic needs and have a visual to process when activities were finished. Once PECs was being used consistently at home and school, Carla's progress increased.

The colour-coded symbols come in sheets of different sizes to suit the child and the situation. They should be available at all times so that pre-verbal children can at least communicate their basic needs. I created a board for every communal area where my class might go. I was told that the symbols would be lost and that I would get tired of replacing them. They did get lost. It was frustrating, but I kept replacing them because I thought if I was pre-verbal and needed a symbol to tell someone I wanted 'help' or needed the 'toilet', I would hope someone would keep replacing my means of communicating these basic needs.

# Chapter 3
# The Visual Timetable

'Not knowing when the dawn will come I open every door.'

Emily Dickinson

Imagine that you are on a jam-packed underground train. There is no map indicating the number of stops. You cannot see out of the window to find which stations are passing by. It is hot and the mixture of body odours is turning your stomach. The air feels thick like it is running out. Voices echo in multiple languages. They sound unfamiliar and aggressive. You want to cover your ears, but cannot because you have to hold on. The ground is wobbling violently. You feel dizzy and overwhelmed. The train screeches to a nails-down-a-blackboard halt. You try to see a station name, but there are multiple foreign signs. What if this is your stop? The doors jerk open. In the distance you see daylight. What would you do?

Relate the feeling of that train journey to how children with autism might feel when they start school. They look around for a visual. They need to know that they are in the right place, what they will be expected to do and how long this will last. The visual needs to be easy to pick out amidst all the other signs, symbols and information. If expectations are clearly displayed, the children can make informed decisions. When we set out on an unfamiliar journey we like to know what the stops will be and how long we are going to be on the train. If the train becomes packed and uncomfortable, we can count down to when we can get off. The destination is our motivator to stay on. We are getting somewhere…

Presenting useful information clearly is so important from the outset. First impressions will be recorded and reactions repeated. Ideally, before the child with autism starts school he will have had a visual explanation of what will happen on the first day. Websites often offer a window into a setting and it is worth printing out pictures so that when the child arrives there are some familiar markers.

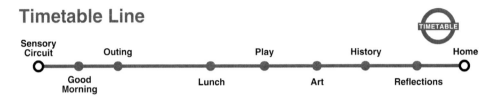

*Figure 3.1 Comparing the child's timetable to an underground map*

Visual timetables and schedules are like underground maps. Those maps not only help people reach a destination, they affect the emotional experience. If we look out of the window and see an unexpected station name, we look for the coloured line relating to our route. We look for that station name on our route and if it's there, we know we are okay. For children with autism, starting the school day without a timetable could be like putting them on a crowded underground train without a map. Without a 'map' they have no idea of how many stops until they get home or how long the experience will last. Time moves incredibly slowly when we are not having fun.

What if these children decide they cannot cope? They look for some way out. Autism-specific schools often have double door handles on the classroom doors. An adult can reach and open both door handles, but a child can't. If the child gets past these, there are a series of locked doors, followed by locked gates. If children know that they cannot physically get out, they may try to zone out instead. They escape by focusing on something that is comforting to them, such as watching sand pour. This may be a coping mechanism. As Carissa Cascio, Assistant Professor of Psychiatry at Vanderbilt University, Tennessee, explains, 'A strong response to high intensity stimuli in autism could be one reason for withdrawal' (Foss-Feig *et al.* 2013).

An adult in the dentist's chair might try to visualise being in a relaxing place, such as a beach. What if visual distraction is not enough though? What if the dentist is drilling and the pain is unbearable? If children cannot find a way to block things out, the next tactic might be disruptive. Will this be flight or fight? They up the level of disruption until either they are allowed to leave or the teacher evacuates the class to keep the other children safe. Children learn the level they had to get to before the lesson was stopped and the next time they don't bother with the build-up. They know it is much faster to go straight to the behaviour that led to the evacuation. These coping strategies can become a sort of habit or learnt behaviour. The child associates the activity with the behaviour and it plays out each time.

We have to try to get things right from the start because these children record experiences and reactions. That is why we need to get in as early as possible with visual supports that show where they are, what they should be doing and how long it will take. Our visual timetable is their underground map supporting them on an intense and sometimes frightening journey. We give the child access to a clear visual timetable mapping the day ahead. We check that every symbol is readable and relates to what we will be doing. If symbols and associations are too complicated for some children, then we break things down to help them understand. If they cannot relate our lessons to the 'literacy' and 'science' symbols, why not simplify them by area – use 'red table' or 'yellow table' (buying new furniture is not necessary as coloured tape, flags or visual markers can be used to differentiate areas). The timetable symbols must be readable to be effective.

*Figure 3.2 Red table and yellow table square symbols*

*Figure 3.3 Cooking at the red table*

*Figure 3.4 Literacy at the yellow table*

*Figure 3.5 Red and green workstations defined by coloured paper*

Photographs can be used on a visual timetable, but they must be very clear or they could be confusing. A photo of the swimming pool should show the school pool, not a public pool with lots of children on a big inflatable. I once taught a child who responded well to photographs that showed her doing things. If she was not in the photo, she did not show any interest. If photographs don't seem enough, then objects of reference can be used that can be matched to an object related to the room you are going to. A paintbrush might represent the art area; a ball pool ball could represent soft play. A child's individual timetable could be made up of a series of objects linked with photographs of different places. Doors to rooms can be painted so that a symbol showing a blue door can be used to show a child where to transition to next. A child might carry a booster seat to the mini bus so that he knows an outing is on the agenda. When going to the swimming pool he takes a swimming bag. We use what makes sense to individual children. We give them the information they need to feel safe in a format they recognise.

It's not that these children can't learn to read. If they stop and really focus, they can – but most of the time they are going too fast. Think of how things blur as a train moves at top speed and we can't read station names as they pass – but when the train stops, we can.

A study at Vanderbilt University revealed that children with autism could see simple movement twice as fast as other children their age. Twenty children with autism and 26 typically developing children aged 8–17 looked at brief video clips of moving black-and-white bars and indicated in which direction the bars were heading – right or left. When the visual bars were given greater contrast, all the children performed better. 'But kids with autism, got much, much better – performing twice as well as their peers' (Foss-Feig *et al.* 2013).

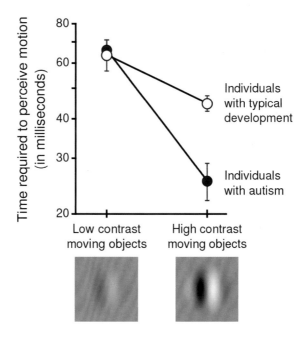

*Figure 3.6 Graph showing that children with autism detect simple movement twice as quickly as their typically developing peers*
Source: Duje Tadin, University of Rochester, New York

Foss-Feig states:

> This dramatically enhanced ability to perceive motion is a hint that the brains of individuals with autism keep responding more and more as intensity increases. Although this could be considered advantageous, in most circumstances if the neural response doesn't stop at the right level it could lead to sensory overload. (Foss-Feig *et al.* 2013)

Observe children with autism engaged in an activity they really love. You may start to see mannerisms that include leaning in to look at things close-up. Watch children with autism playing a computer game they enjoy. Often they will zoom in, delighting in seeing every detail, perhaps flapping their hands or twiddling their fingers (often referred to as 'stimming'). This might be helping their concentration. When they are most intensely engaged with something, they might look more 'autistic'. Mannerisms such as leaning in and flicking fingers can show that the child is really enjoying the moment.

The child may bounce with sheer delight while replaying a favourite scene on a DVD – the joy of learning how to use the rewind button! Why do autistic children do this? Is it another way of skipping to what's important? They know the film by heart, but what they want to see is that bit that makes them truly happy or that they do not understand. They watch it again and again, and it becomes a habit – like a 'stim'.

A recent study revealed that when copying the actions that an adult modelled, children with autism were more likely to skip the 'silly' or unnecessary steps. The study involved 31 children with autism and 30 typically developing children. The children watched as an adult showed them how to remove a toy from a closed plastic box. Some steps were necessary, such as unclipping the lid and taking it off. Other steps were unnecessary, such as tapping the lid twice. The children were given the container and asked to get the toy out as quickly as they could. The children with autism were much less likely to copy the unnecessary steps than their typically developing peers. Antonia Hamilton, of the University of Nottingham in England, said in a statement: 'Autistic children only do the actions they really need to do.' Previous studies have shown that children with autism are less likely to catch contagious yawning. They do not feel the need to copy social steps that are pointless in order to fit in (Marsh *et al.* 2013).

Knowing this makes me wonder what would happen if we gave the child with autism a magic remote control for life – which bits would he rewind to and replay? Would many of our daily routines be seen as an unnecessary step? Would the child sit and listen to a story if it were possible to fast forward to computer time? We can't provide these children with a remote control, but we can give them information to help them navigate the day.

The child must be able to find important information amidst visual clutter. Adding colour to symbols makes these easier to spot in the environment. Colours that are visually appealing will catch the autistic child's eye. Children with autism like matching colour to colour and cracking our colour codes – these things make sense. For example, if they want to know what we are doing next, they look for purple. They can then stop and zoom in for a closer look to check the details.

*Figure 3.7 A visual timetable*

We know that adding colour codes to information makes things easier to find fast. That's why we colour code cleaning equipment, rubbish bins and road signs. Once you start looking, you'll see colour codes are used everywhere because they stand out in the environment.

## Individual schedules

Children may benefit from having an individual timetable tailored to their day. If they have a one-to-one speech therapy session during the day, we need to show them this so they don't think we have made a mistake.

Colour helps to sort lots of information into an understandable order. Many people with autism naturally tune in to colour codes. Colours communicate. When we are on the underground and know we are travelling on the northern line, we look for the black line. If our route to work involves the underground, we will soon learn the route without being so reliant on the colour-coded maps. The colours break things down so we have a starting point.

We can help create connections between an individual timetable and the class timetable by using the same colour. If we mount individual schedules onto the same colour as the class timetable, children can connect their individual timetable with the class timetable.

## 'Now' and 'next'

Sometimes a whole day is too much to take in. We can break the day down to meet children's individual needs. They might start off with a 'now' and 'next' or 'first' and 'then' visual and move onto 'now', 'next' and 'later'. The 'now' and 'next' board might start off with an activity followed by a reward. The activity would be further broken down with tokens for each part completed.

*Figure 3.8 A visual timetable above a 'now' and 'next' board*

The 'now' picture on the 'now' and 'next' board should somehow link with the main class timetable. If the child responds better to photographs or visuals, such as 'red table' instead of 'science', make sure you add these visuals to your class timetable so he can make a connection. You may show the class science symbol with a connector symbol or symbols below it. If all the children will be at the red table, show this. If you will split the group between the red and yellow tables, then add both.

## Timetable changes

We know that children with autism often enjoy memorising things that do not change. We must take care not to present the timetable as unchangeable or they will memorise it and be anxious when it goes wrong.

How do we introduce the idea that things will sometimes change? We show from the start that the timetable can change. The first time a day repeats, change something. Stick to a timetable of lessons, but swap things about a bit. One week have a story before playtime and the next week have a snack. This way the child does not create a set-in-stone picture of the whole day.

If you were to change part of the timetable without any warning and you have never done this before, it may seem to autistic children that you have torn up their perfect picture of the day. You've not only disrupted their routine, but caused confusion and created distrust. If you changed one activity, the pattern is different and they know that you could change anything. You could even cancel lunch. Changing the timetable is like a great big warning alarm bell if they have learnt it as a set fact. It's not necessarily about a need for routine, but a need to *know* that the day is on the right track and that they are still on the right 'train'.

Do some children with autism want the same thing for lunch every day because they cannot cope with change? Or is it because they have found something that works – that is, they have recorded the information, they will not be forced to rethink it and they can move on to the next thing? Do they like order because it means they can think about something more important? Think of adults who always dress the same or have the same lunch every day. Is this because they are rigid or is it because they do not want to waste brain power and time thinking about what to wear or eat when they have already found things that are okay. Appearance and food are not a priority when you're busy working out how to split an atom. The strategies we use with autistic children are like safety nets supporting them, allowing them free time for their pursuit of truth.

Do change things, but try to keep changes positive. It's so easy to get stuck doing the same thing because it keeps things level and consistent. But this is not setting the child up to succeed in life, because things do change without warning all the time.

## A 'whoops!'

Introduce the idea of a 'whoops!' on the timetable as soon as possible. This is when something has to change unexpectedly. Don't wait for an actual 'whoops!' to occur, but plan it. Please see Chapter 13 for more information on handling a 'whoops' and preparing for a fire drill.

## Carousel lessons

The arrow circles at the corners of the symbol are added to show a 'swippy swappy' lesson (times when you are going to split the group). There may be turn-taking games on the red table and handwriting at the green table. A class may split, so half of them will be at soft play and the other half are doing literacy. Adding this little symbol teaches the child that when you start doing literacy and half the children leave for soft play, it's okay. He will still get to go to soft play. Without these symbols the class timetable would seem wrong to half of the children. It could also seem unfair. We explain because we understand that the child needs to know. Visual explanations show children that we respect that they need to know.

*Figure 3.9 Carousel symbols on the timetable show when groups will swap*

## Show and tell

We must constantly try to see the visuals through the eyes of the individual, often literal child. Imagine if you could not read the words. Does each symbol *show* what the next activity is going to be?

I once taught a child who had a history of having meltdowns on days when sausages were on the menu. She was a vegetarian. Was it because she loved sausages and could not have them? Looking at the class visual timetable revealed a possible reason. The lunchtime symbol showed a plate of food (sausages and peas). Every day she had been shown a sausages symbol, but there were no sausages. Then the one day there were sausages at lunchtime she could not have them because she was vegetarian. I changed the sausage symbol to one that showed sandwiches and the next day she tried to take another child's sandwich. These children can be so literal. It's vital we look at the visuals and try to see them through their eyes. We decided to trial a symbol that showed a selection of options in order to demonstrate that lunch could be a number of different things. I couldn't find a symbol that showed this, which meant making one. This child made me re-evaluate all the timetable symbols by looking at them literally. I realised that many of our symbols could confuse or misinform in the same way.

*Figure 3.10 Sausage symbol, sandwich symbol and new 'lunch' symbol*

Another child I taught in the past would always ask for a ball at playtime, but as soon as he got one he would throw it up on the roof or over the fence. The timetable symbol for playtime showed a child throwing a ball up in the air. Could the visual have been at the root of this learnt behaviour?

We know these children can be visual and literal. Having a symbol is not enough. We must have visuals that communicate and do not confuse.

I started looking at all the other symbols we were using. Our science symbol showed a test tube, yet we had never used test tubes in science. What if children were utterly reliant on this visual? It bore no relation to what the children do in science. How would it help them? We adapted the science symbol to show three things we might associate with science lessons – a magnet, a lightbulb and a leaf. The idea was to show variety and the type of things we might do in science. We then applied this principle to all the other timetable symbols. As well as helping children to understand what we might be teaching during sessions, these tailored subject symbols may also help children to generalise.

## Using schedules with transition boards

The children are given their photos with their names on to match to their individual schedules. They go to their schedule and remove the first symbol. They take this symbol and place it on a board in that area (see Figure 10.5).

If a child has an individual schedule, he can use the symbols from it to help learn to make transitions between activities in different areas. The child learns to check his schedule. You may give him his photo or name to match to the schedule to indicate it is time for him to check it. He goes to check his schedule and sees that the next symbol is 'red table'. He physically removes the symbol. (The symbols are best laminated and attached to the schedule with velcro.) The child then takes his 'red table' symbol and goes to the red table. On the red table there is a purple transition board with a timetable size 'red table' symbol in the centre. The child sees other small 'red table' schedule size symbols placed on the board. He places his symbol on the board. This visual helps with the physical transition by removing the need to process lots of language and giving him a task (placing the symbol) to focus on.

A short schedule or 'now' and 'next' board can be a stepping stone towards using a longer individual schedule. The child learns to place his larger 'red table' symbol matching the one at the centre of the transition board.

Some teachers colour code these symbols so that if a child is not reading the symbols, he can use colour as a guide. If the child is not yet reading lesson symbols, use a symbol that he will understand for transitions, such as a red table. This means the child is a step closer to reading symbols. As children progress, they will match their name and they will learn to 'read' lesson symbols. In time they may be able to follow a typed schedule and tick things off or cross them out as they are completed. The colours are a stepping stone. The aim is that the need for a visual timetable will fade over time.

Also think about breaking down transitions in the day. If it's your intention that children will change for PE or swimming, it may be worth including the changing room on the schedule before and after the activity and having a transition board for the changing room. We cannot assume that the children will see the changing room as a natural step in the PE lesson. Getting changed can also be an issue in itself and it is better that the children are forewarned.

Purple is a colour often associated with authority. We use this when we want a child to follow a timetabled activity. Our expectation when using purple symbols is that the child will follow their direction. There is also an option to make the timetable symbols into arrow shapes to further illustrate movement and direction. Autistic children often tune in to shape as well as to colour. Shaping symbols can tune in to shape interest and gives an extra visual clue when children are seeking important information fast.

When I enter a classroom, I zoom in on the visuals. We must constantly assess them. Do they make sense? Could they mislead if taken literally? Do they paint the best possible picture for the visual learner? It is better to have no visual than one that will confuse. Compare the children's visuals to lifesaving rings. They must be quick to locate and understand if they are to be of any use during a crisis or sensory overload. Visuals are not just for show or to tick a strategy box. Having these symbols can make a huge difference to a student's experience of education, aiding understanding and reducing anxiety.

# Chapter 4
# Time Trackers

Time is important to people with autism. Before they can read clocks they often look for ways to work out time. We are not born knowing how to tell the time using clocks, but people with autism often have a need to know the time. Before we had clocks, sunlight and shadows were the means of telling time. Could some children with autism be using light and shadows to work out how to measure time? Kristine Barnett explains that is exactly what her son Jake did. As a baby 'Jake could spend hours watching the play of light and shadows.'

Daniel Tammet recalls:

> As I sat still and silent hour after hour, I diligently watched the wash of different hues and colours ebb and flow across the walls and furniture of my room with the day's passage; the flow of time made visual. (Tammet 2007, p.73)

We also know that Isaac Newton had an early obsession with sundials and learnt to tell the time using light and shadows.

*Figure 4.1 Isaac Newton had an early fascination with sundials*

Visual timers allow us to show time passing. Timers explain how long an activity is going to last and are also visual reminders that an enjoyable activity will have to end at some point. They are predictable, fixed, and for this reason they are calming. There are many types of visual timer now available.

*Figure 4.2 A traffic light timer, small time timer and egg timer*

If the timetable does not show how long an activity will last, children with autism may feel they have no control. Go back to that busy train crammed with people. You could tolerate 20 minutes, but an hour would be too much. You might use the number of stops and count down. The station names tell us that we are getting closer to our stop. Compare this to how autistic children may feel, sitting on the carpet for a story. They need to know how long they are going to be sitting. If they have not been shown this on a timer, they will try to create their own visual markers. You have shown them a 'good sitting' symbol, so they know what you want them to do, but you have not shown them 'how long'. Is the 'good sitting' going to be for the whole day? They try to work it out for themselves by seeking a visual clue and decide that when the teacher closes the book it will be the end. They use the pages turning as a sort of timer counting down to the end of the uncomfortable sitting lesson. The book closes and everyone stays seated. The teacher starts asking questions about the story. Suddenly there is no end in sight. The child feels that he is in a big, unknown ocean with no clue how long this sitting lesson will last. The child starts to feel uncomfortable and out of control and might fidget or get up. He is very unlikely to be processing the teacher's questions so will not be keeping up with what the rest of the class is doing.

Learning to use a clock will not be instant, but we can use colour to help decode the language associated with telling the time and give the classroom clock a makeover with some coloured paper.

*Figure 4.3 Colour-coded classroom clock using coloured paper*

Access to visual timers can really help people with autism stay on the 'train' because they know how long the journey is expected to last. It will also mean that, instead of working out the time and the length of the 'sitting', they might be able to learn something during the lesson.

Having to sit for too long can be really distracting to the child who has a sensory need to bounce. If we are aware that a child finds sitting difficult, why not let him get up and have a jump about at times? We cannot know how much energy it takes to sit still because to us it comes naturally. A child will get more out of the lesson if his physical and emotional needs are respected.

Egg timers are often colour coded according to how long they last. Teachers learn to link the colour of the timer to the right amount of time. They know, for example, that the purple timer is 15 minutes. If they are used regularly, it is possible the child will learn to link the length of time it takes for the sand to go through with a particular coloured egg timer.

Advantages of timers are that children with autism often enjoy watching the sand pour. It can have a calming effect. This can be really good if children need to wind down. They can, of course, get so fixated on the sand that they tune in to that and not to anything else. This is fine during 'rest time', but not during a lesson. Daniel Tammet recalls how at nursery he had 'an obsession with hourglasses (the nursery had several of different sizes) and I remember watching the trickling flow of sand over and over again, oblivious to the children playing around me' (Tammet 2007, p.24). Another disadvantage of egg timers is that they can be broken or reset. The reality is that, despite the best intentions, the timer may not get used regularly enough.

*Figure 4.4 Colour-coded egg timers*

Verbal countdowns can be effective. We say there are five minutes left at the park. The child might respond to this well, but the 'five minutes' has to be consistent. We cannot say five minutes and then allow 15 minutes. We can also use 'Five, four, three, two, one, park is finished.'

There are times when a visual timer or countdown will not work. When watching a DVD, the autistic child may become a part of that film's world and will expect to carry on watching until the credits roll at the end. If this is not possible, do not start the film. Choose an activity that fits into the time you have. If we switch something off that the child is engaged with before it is finished, he may react in an extreme way. Be aware that if the autistic child is absorbed in something he will not want it to end. When using computers or watching television, agree a structured 'finish' before it starts. Stick to the plan. The child might try to renegotiate, but will actually feel safer if you remain consistent. With computers and TV it is better to agree to switch off at the end of the programme or pause at a certain level of a game than to use a timer –if a timer went off two minutes before the end of a programme you would not want it switched off.

Our visual timetable is so important. For some children it's a bit like a lifeline. I wanted to find a way to show them how long each lesson would last. It had to be visual, consistent and non-distracting. Could we make a symbol to represent the timers and show how long we expect each lesson to be?

We can let a child see how long a lesson will be without the distraction of watching sand pour, by adding visual timer symbols to our timetable symbols. For example, if lunchtime is always 30 minutes, we could add a visual of three orange ten-minute timers above the lunch symbol.

*Figure 4.5 Timetable with orange egg timers*

Using symbols of coloured egg timers helps the child make associations, removes the physical problem of turning the timer over once it is finished and creates a visual display that explains that some timetabled activities will last longer than others.

The coloured symbols must be the same as the amount of time the coloured egg timer takes. We should also show the child the actual egg timer to help him make the link. Start with one colour of timer (the one which relates to the set amount of time for your shortest session) to avoid creating confusion. If you have an orange, ten-minute timer, break blocks of time down into ten minutes. The good thing about using the symbols is that they are fixed and a child will not try to turn them over.

If a child needs a visual to know what stage he has reached in the day, you could remove the timers as the day goes on. If you are going to do this,

I'd suggest doing it as each session ends rather than at ten-minute intervals, because ten-minute intervals are easy to miss. Or you could remove symbols and timers as each session ends and post them in a 'finished' postbox. Doing this could even be 'sold' as a reward.

Another visual way of showing time on the timetable is to add visuals based on time timers. These timers use the colour red to show time in blocks, and relate to the clock face. As time passes, the red section gets smaller.

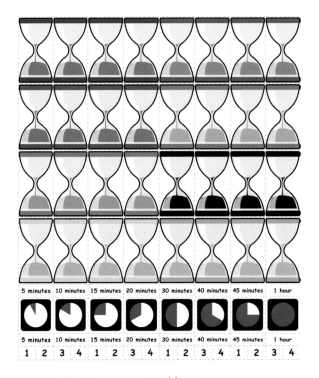

Figure 4.6 A timetable timer resource

Figure 4.7 A timetable with red time timer symbols

*Figure 4.8 A time timer with 'now' and 'next' and timer symbols*

People with autism often like order. While other children are racing their toy cars, the autistic child might line them up and get a sense of calm from having them in the right place. Naoki Higashida, a 13-year-old Japanese boy with autism, explains that 'people with autism memorise things because it's fun'. Train timetables, birthdates, number plates and historic dates are fixed and this gives them a simplicity which can be comforting to someone who is autistic. 'The number 1 is only ever the number 1' (Higashida 2013).

We must take care that our visual timetables do not become fixed and that we regularly include changes to the routine. The children must know from the outset that daily activities can change, otherwise they may go into a state of panic when something is not the same. By constructing a changeable picture, we will avoid causing any distress later on because the children learn that the order of events is not necessarily fixed.

These children become fixed on the things that make most sense and feel secure with sameness. An autistic child might have a meltdown if you change the route to school if it has previously been the same every day. By keeping things the same when they could potentially change in the future, we are creating false security systems that can cause almighty problems when they fail.

Our timetable is so central to the children's day and it should be ordered to create a sense of calm. Symbols should be the same size and each one must make sense so that when the children zoom in for a look, it is worthwhile. The more perfect we can make our timetable, the more it will 'speak' to children with autism. It should be the first thing we focus on getting right, because creating order calms, comforts and makes the children feel safe. The more information we can provide with the visual timetable about the day, the more we set the children up to succeed.

I have been trying to see through the visual learners' eyes for so long because I know that getting things just right is the key to teaching them. Now when I see a higgledy-piggledy jumble of symbols that don't make sense on a visual timetable, I can literally feel the autistic child's discomfort. These children deserve better. Let's give them the order they crave, the attention to detail they enjoy. If you speak their language when explaining what you have planned for the day, they are more likely to see it as an achievable journey. Look at how perfectly these children often line up their toys. Our visual timetable should mirror this attention to detail. Getting an answer often depends on how we present a question. We have to make them want to answer. There always has to be a point. Create a calm day by presenting the order of events in a clear way from the very start.

If you get the timetable right from the outset, children with autism may decide they can try to stay on the learning train.

# Chapter 5

# Colour Categories

'He who loves practice without theory is like the sailor
who boards ship without a rudder and compass
and never knows where he may cast.'

Leonardo Da Vinci

To explain colour categories we must get back on that fast-moving underground train. Imagine that when you look for the station sign there are 20 similar signs (all the same colour and style). None of them really mean anything to you because they are written in a foreign language. You need to know if this is your station. That is all you need to know. Other signs might say 'toilets', 'way out' or 'good sitting', but right now this information is insignificant. They are causing visual clutter which is hiding the information you need. Compare this to looking for a word in a dictionary that is not ordered alphabetically.

What if, before you got on the train, someone told you that the signs were colour coded? Station names were always outlined with purple? You do not need to read and translate every sign. The information you need will be purple. The colour code provides a fast way to sort a visual jumble. It increases our chances of finding relevant information fast.

Colour communicates faster than words or black-and-white pictures. By adding colour we can help group our visuals so that when we present them it's immediately clear whether our request is personal care (washing hands, having a bath, etc.) or related to good behaviour (sharing a toy or space).

Picture yourself standing at a bus stop, waiting for a bus. Traffic passes so fast it's a visual blur. Buses only stop for seconds. The buses each have a number, but they are moving too fast to read numbers. By the time you have read and processed the number, the bus has gone. What if you knew that if you got on the yellow bus, it would take you home? Even at speed we can single out colours and remember the code. Colour communicates fast.

*Figure 5.1 Symbols without colour codes are visually confusing and take longer to locate*

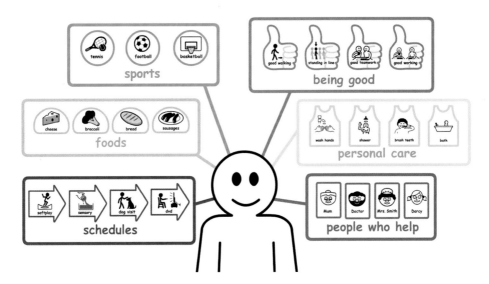

*Figure 5.2 Colour-coded symbols help to sort visual clutter*

Connecting colours can help children with autism draw on learnt experiences and generalise, which may reduce their anxiety.

Temple Grandin explains: 'When you think visually, and you don't have much stuff on the [mental] hard drive from previous experiences, you've got to have something to use as a visual map' (Grandin 2011, p.xxxiii).

*Figure 5.3 A messy pile of clothes*

*Figure 5.4 An ordered wardrobe*

Look at the pile of clothes in Figure 5.3 and the order that can be created using categories and colour to organise them (Figure 5.4). Transfer these images to the mind of the autistic child. These children have all this information, but they need a way to sort it out. Colour coding can help clarify by providing visual structure.

## Personal care

Washing hands is something we teach children because it removes germs, stops the spread of bacteria and reduces the likelihood of us getting ill. However, a child with autism may just not accept the need for hand washing. This social norm might seem bizarre and without reason to him, so why conform?

To the autistic child, contact with water may be an uncomfortable sensation. Perhaps at one time the water was too hot or he may associate hand washing with the presence of noisy hand driers. When children refuse to wash their hands, we may not know all the connections they are making. Children with autism remember and record experiences – particularly if they have caused sensory discomfort.

Naoki Higashida explains:

> When memories suddenly come back to people we experience a flashback, but in the case of people with autism memories are not stored in a clear order. For those of us who are disturbed by having our hair and nails trimmed, somehow their negative memories are probably connected to the action.
>
> A normal person might say, 'Oh. He's never liked having his hair cut or his nails trimmed ever since he was small, but we've no idea why'.
>
> The thing is, the memory of a person with autism isn't like a number scale from which you pick out the recollection you are after. It's more like a jigsaw puzzle where if even one piece is mis-inserted the entire puzzle becomes impossible to complete. What's more a single piece that doesn't belong there can mess up all the surrounding memories as well. So it's not necessarily physical pain that's making us cry at all. Quite possibly it's memory. (Higashida 2013, pp.87–88)

So we use visuals, model that it is okay, build up good experiences and help the child understand the reasons behind washing hands and cutting nails. Reasons are important. It might seem clear to us why we do these things, but a visual explanation will help the child with autism. Take care not to be too extreme in the explanation though or you could set the child up to become obsessive about washing hands. The correct balance will depend on the individual child. Once we have got past this and the child learns to cope with washing hands, it becomes part of his daily routine The child accepts it and somehow overcomes what was causing the anxiety.

*Figure 5.5 A 'wash hands' visual*

Let's move on to the next hurdle – washing hair, for example. Autistic children may not be able to transfer learning about hand hygiene to the body and hair. Washing hair might seem new and frightening. Again, these children may be making associations we are unaware of. They might have no idea of why we want them to wash their hair. But if they could connect washing their hair with a conquered fear or accepted routine (e.g. washing hands), we would gain valuable ground. To help them make the link we can provide a visual structure.

By using a colour code we can provide the child with a visual link for self-help skills. As a starting point, the self-help/health and hygiene symbols created for this study were surrounded by a bathroom-inspired aqua. Because children with autism can be very particular about colour, you may want to cut out the symbols and outline or mount them on a colour of the child's choice. The colour does not matter, but being consistent is vital.

Figure 5.6 'Wash hands' and 'wash hair' visuals linked by colour

The hope is that when children see the 'wash hair' symbol they will make an immediate connection with the 'wash hands' visual. The colour triggers memories and helps them build associations. We provide a visual way for them to create a category for personal care activities. The children build a bank of conquered fears, which helps them to overcome future hurdles. It is hoped that this will provide a balance when they associate a painful memory.

Figure 5.7 'Wash hands', 'wash hair' and 'brush teeth' visuals linked by colour

Colour coding gives children a specific area or 'drawer' for health and hygiene. When faced with a related challenge, they should be able to recall their own personal experience and recall previous lessons learnt.

*Figure 5.8 'Wash hands' and 'wash hair' visuals going into an aqua-coloured drawer*

As children progress, you could highlight, underline or use a coloured pen to code their schedule. So, for example, as they get older and we plan to introduce them to using a deodorant, we highlight 'deodorant' with an aqua-coloured pen when we add it to their morning schedule. The ability to link by using colour will immediately tell them it's one of those things you do to be healthy or hygienic. They can process and categorise this new request without lots of language. We will have given them a lot of learnt personal, historical information just by linking our new request with the familiar colour. We may also lessen the anxiety and fear sometimes associated with learning new self-help skills.

As I began to think about updating and coding our symbols, it occurred to me that we could further distinguish them for visual learners by adding relevant shapes. Naoki Higashida describes how, 'When a colour is vivid or a shape is eye-catching that's the detail that catches our attention, and then our hearts kind of drown in it, and we can't concentrate on anything else' (Higashida 2013, p.92).

We know that getting children's attention is half the battle. So we can use the power of colours and shapes to grab their attention and get them to focus in on the visual. We know these children are more likely to learn when we motivate. It's like meeting them halfway.

Symbols do not have to be square. Personal care symbols can be vest-shaped (a unisex item of personal clothing). We could add an element of fun to schedules by using a washing line and pegs. As parts of a schedule are completed, they could be put in a washing basket ('finished').

*Figure 5.9 A washing line sequence (the symbols can be taken off the line and put into the washing basket as steps are completed)*

## Colour codes for behaviour and social skills

We know that children with autism respond well to visual instructions and that they notice the details in their surrounding environment. If I change one symbol on my class timetable, I can guarantee a student will come in, notice immediately and ask me why.

It is helpful to display desired behaviour in a visual way – for example, 'good sitting', 'good sharing' or 'good walking'. The image should show the children exactly what we want to see and be specific to time. We must be careful not to cause any confusion for the literal learner. We should not, for example, show a 'good sitting' symbol with a child sat on a chair if we are asking him to sit nicely on the floor.

Using a colour code for behaviour and social situations allows children to build another category or 'drawer'. It adds to the visual and helps them store and retrieve more useful information.

By highlighting or linking the visual with a colour, we allow the children to seek out these cues in their environment as they are needed. They may be thinking, 'I don't know how to behave', so we could teach them to look for the visual. We can reinforce that these symbols show desired behaviours by pointing to them when we give praise or rewards. For example, you could say 'Good turn-taking, Charlie', and hold up/point to the turn-taking image. This way, the child who may not have processed the language will be able to see what you are giving praise for. As time goes on he will connect the positives and praise with children doing the things on the orange cards and may start to copy those positive behaviours to get praise.

Will children become too reliant on these visuals? The short answer is 'No'. We use behaviour charts and reward systems to motivate children to learn to behave or take part. In time we adapt/reduce the rewards and up our expectations. Having the correct behaviours and social skills shown visually helps children learn, and in time they will associate the activity with the desired behaviour.

*Figure 5.10 A big thumbs-up for 'good walking'*

Our positive social behaviour visuals have an orange outline. They can be printed on a traditional square or on a thumbs-up shape. Why should symbols be square when we can shape them to communicate even more? If these symbols are more effective I don't think people will mind taking the extra time to cut them out. They are quick to locate when the child wonders how we are expecting him to behave. They also create a positive atmosphere.

These symbols are for display in areas where we are likely to want to see these particular behaviours. We want them to stand out. We want to be able to point to them and show children that they are doing well. The visual examples show children what we want to see them doing. If they are acting like the visual (e.g. walking down the corridor), we must reinforce this with praise. Let children know that by copying the picture they are getting it right. Maybe they will glance at the thumbs-up and recall that type of behaviour getting a good reaction. They might just test it to see if it still works. If we see the positive behaviour, we must always show that reaction.

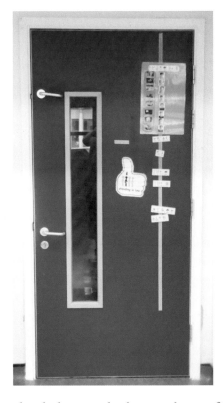

*Figure 5.11 A thumb shape on the door can be seen from a distance*

*Figure 5.12 This thumb-shaped visual is for 'good standing in line'*

The children can see the positive thumbs-up on the door from a distance when they are lining up. They can then 'zoom in' to see the behaviour expectation.

The behaviour symbols can also be printed small and used as tokens. This means the child can actually see all the positive reasons for them. We can colour code token boards to link with what the focus is. If they are for good behaviour (and this can include good working), we can add them to an orange token board.

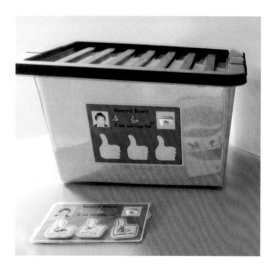

*Figure 5.13 A behaviour token board and a reward box full of motivators*

Children need to know our expectations and what we are rewarding. If we have an orange board, they will know to look for those orange visual cues for how they should behave. Our focus is orange behaviour and that will earn them the reward. We can still relate this to lessons showing them the token so they know they are working, for example, for their 'good cutting' token.

There are also different types of 'good working' symbols, so you can show exactly what you hope to see. There's an image for children working as a team, working independently and working independently sat next to each other. It's so important to show them exactly what we want to see. A single 'good working' symbol is not enough. I also prefer a 'work' symbol that does not show a child writing, because children with autism can have real difficulties with writing due to the need for instant perfection or constraints of their fine-motor skills. Matching is often a strong point for visual learners and a more likely starting point. For this reason we changed the 'working' symbol to show the figure matching.

*Figure 5.14 Work symbols showing how we expect the child to work*

You can print these token boards onto card from our resources CD-ROM or make a reward board with orange card.

*Figure 5.15 A behaviour reward board*

The tokens show the children what our expectation is. It is good to show them what the next token will be for, in order to clarify our expectations.

The children learn that if they are unsure of what to do, they can look for an orange thumbs-up visual cue. As time goes on, these positives will be recorded in memory and stored neatly in their metaphorical social behaviour drawer.

*Figure 5.16 Sorting requests into the orange behaviour drawer*

Orange is often used in marketing aimed at children because they are naturally drawn towards this colour. It is also the colour used for lifeboats and helpful indicators of a hazard, as in road cones. These behaviour symbols could act as lifeboats because they allow autistic children to see how they are expected to behave in a situation. With a visual they can negotiate a difficult situation because they have something to cling to. These symbols quietly and clearly show the child our expectations.

## Careful colours for foods

Food can be a huge issue for children with autism. We all want to see our children get their five a day. We want them to have a varied diet to help them grow strong and develop healthy eating habits. It can be heartbreaking to watch children refuse to eat anything but dry bread rolls or cereal. We know it's not good for them, but they refuse to move on. By allocating a colour code to foods we give them a group. Rather than seeing the foods they will eat as totally isolated, they begin to see them as part of a family. As we introduce new foods, the child might like them.

The beige colour code I have chosen for 'foods' relates to the bread and cereal that are so often the starting point in the autistic child's repertoire of foods. These symbols could also be shaped like bread rolls (see Figure 5.18) to create another link.

*Figure 5.17 Creating a category for foods with colour*

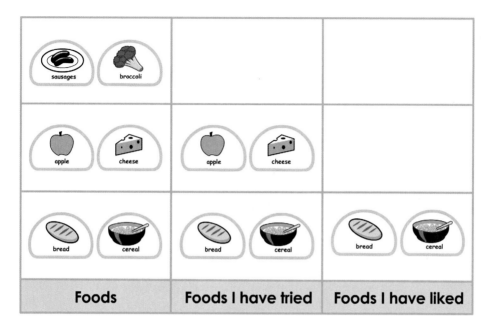

*Figure 5.18 Foods in categories*

Because food can be such a huge issue for people with autism, select colours for these symbols with care. All the colour-coded symbols in this book can also be printed in black and white, allowing colour codes to be suited to the child. There would be little point in colour coding all the food symbols/ words in beige if the individual indicated a dislike of that colour.

## Why are visuals often more effective?

Using visuals can help many children with autism make sense of our requests and allow them time to process. There's that old saying, 'A picture speaks a thousand words.' A spoken request may be misunderstood and warrants a faster, more urgent response. Think of asking a child to go to the toilet when he is watching television. You've seen that tell-tale wiggle and you *know* the child needs the toilet. If you ask him to go to the toilet, the response will be an immediate 'No' (a defence mechanism). But if you show a picture of the toilet, the child might start thinking about it by himself – this might result in a more measured response next time you suggest the child goes to the toilet during a break. The response to verbal requests can often be defensive and without thought. It's like swatting a bee away, mistakenly assuming that it is an annoying fly.

Verbal requests can be an annoying interruption to the child who is deep in thought and he may not even attempt to process them. If someone is in the middle of adding up accounts on a calculator or measuring ingredients for a recipe, we wait for an appropriate time before interrupting because we don't want to disrupt their flow. By waiting we allow the person time to finish the calculation. We do this out of empathy and courtesy. So when we approach the child with a request, we should assume the same. We may not see a calculator, but the child might be deeply engaged in working something out and not take kindly to being interrupted.

So we use symbols or pictures and the person gets a longer time to process. It's not about the understanding, but about the approach... Visuals help. This approach is mostly accepted, so it is time to ensure our symbols and our visuals are perfect. We can bring more order to the visuals so that associated memories are easier to retrieve. Temple Grandin explains, 'Being autistic, I don't naturally assimilate information that most people take for granted. I store information in my head as if it were on a CD-ROM disc. When I recall something I have learnt I replay the video in my imagination' (Grandin 2006, p.8). We give each request a colour-coded category and, if we really want to step outside the box, we can add meaningful shapes.

When teaching a child with autism, most people will agree that adding something we know will motivate the child is a good starting point. This might be a bus, a ball, Mr Potato Head's feet. We do whatever we can to engage the child and open the door. Over time I've noticed that colour and shapes are often motivating. Not only do they create order, but people with autism seem to be tuned in to them.

# Chapter 6
# Social and Emotional Colours

'I can calculate the motion of heavenly bodies,
but not the madness of people.'

Isaac Newton

Children with autism are constantly testing and pursuing truth. They are a bundle of contradictions. They love order and routine, yet often have the most amazingly creative and inventive minds. They may appear to follow rules, but are also the most likely people to come up with a revolutionary new idea. They feel emotion intensely, but often seem to struggle to read facial expressions.

Children with autism are forever experimenting. They might start out trying to work out capacity or relating time to the way shadows fall. Their early experiments can also be social. Could some of the challenging behaviours that often partner autism begin as experiments on measuring human reactions? Are these children exploring boundaries – seeing what makes the toy squeak or the adult shriek? Where another child might accept it when his parent says, 'I love you', the autistic child might view this as a scientific hypothesis. What do scientists do? They conduct thorough tests before drawing conclusions. Once they have completed their tests and accept that the parent's love *is* unconditional, they can feel safe and move on to the next experiment. The most likely target for social testing is usually the person who is with them throughout the day. This person may not have experience of children with autism, but if she loves and keeps showing love, she will have a chance of passing this test. If she gives inconsistent, confusing or exciting reactions, the child will continue to test. Even the most loving, even-tempered, kind-hearted parent will at times be driven to distraction by these experiments. The home that was once a sanctuary has become an arena. The lounge is a battleground and control is up for grabs.

A sibling comes along and the testing may begin all over again. The older child wants to know that the unconditional love he was so sure of has not been diluted. Pre-school starts and there is a whole new set of adults to test. If you want to achieve the best outcomes when teaching children with autism, the first thing you must do is love them. When they know they are loved, they feel most secure.

The children must be sure of you and your reactions. They must feel that you can see their point of view, empathise with things they find hard and be excited by what they love. Then they may accept you as their learning partner. 'The best teachers teach from the heart and not from the book' (Anon). If children with autism get a teacher who loves them as they are, then they will really *want* to learn.

Everything is more intense for these children. If children with autism decide to love dinosaurs, they really, really love everything about them. They might learn all the dinosaur names and want to totally immerse themselves in a dinosaur world. They will do anything to get another dinosaur toy. They will not give up until they get what they want. Tests are intense and rigorous. These children *need* to know every detail. By understanding and supporting this thirst for knowledge, we build children's trust and make them feel safe.

## Carol Gray's Comic Strip Conversations

Comic Strip Conversations were developed by Carol Gray to help individuals with autism develop greater social understanding, and they can be a great starting point when we need to unravel 'incidents'. Simple stick figures are drawn to represent individuals, and only significant key features that were part of the issue are included. Characters are given speech or thought bubbles.

Using Comic Strip Conversations can be highly effective as it allows the child to zoom in and focus on a visual story map of a situation without too much language getting in the way. The stick people represent the child and the other characters, but by drawing the situation it becomes 2D and seems safer to discuss and easier to decode.

The Comic Strip Conversations can also be a good way of illustrating that sometimes what people think and say are different. A visual really helps to explain complex social interactions.

Comic Strip Conversations use symbols to represent social interactions and abstract aspects of conversation. Gray suggests that 'colour may be incorporated to suggest the emotional content of statements, thoughts and questions' (Gray 1994, p.1). The children have access to an assortment of coloured pens which they use to represent different emotions for speech and thoughts. The chosen colour reveals the children's perception of the emotions and this can quickly highlight if there are any misperceptions within the sequence of events and open the door to discussion and clarification.

We list the colours and let the children assign the meaning. I asked our two sons to link colours to their emotions. They were very definite and surprisingly different. The colours we link with emotions are personal and are based on our own preferences, experiences and intuition. They can also be changeable.

| Colour for writing | Malachy (7) | Donovan (5) |
|---|---|---|
| Bad ideas, anger, unfriendly. | Red | Dark Grey |
| Sad or uncomfortable | Blue | Yellow |
| Proud | Gold | Blue |
| Frightened | Dark Brown | Red |
| Facts and truth | Green | Green |
| Comfortable & cosy | Yellow | Golden |
| Questions | Turquoise | Silver |
| Confusion | Pink | Orange |

*Figure 6.1 How children link different colours to feelings*

In Figure 6.2 we were reflecting on what happened one hot summer's day. Malachy wanted to fill the paddling pool, but instead of pointing the hose into the pool he was spraying it in the air. Grandpa and the other children were not impressed. Malachy was cross too because he had chosen a different way, which appealed to his sense of mischief. He could not really see the problem because he was having a wonderful time and some of the water was still going in the pool. I asked what he was thinking and he said with a big smile, 'I was thinking "be crazy".' Malachy chose to assign red to angry words and blue to sad words.

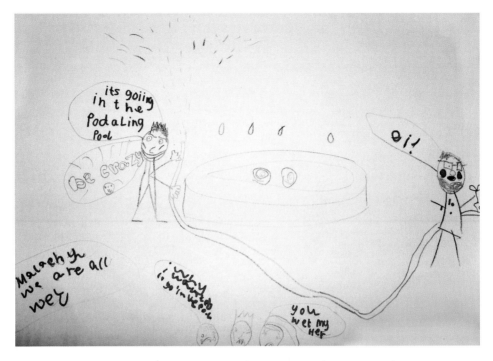

*Figure 6.2 A comic strip showing water being sprayed into the air instead of into the paddling pool*

This drawing prompted a reflective conversation about how the other children were feeling. We were able to discuss how, although Malachy enjoyed the feeling of 'being crazy', no one else was enjoying it and that if he had filled the pool efficiently, all the children could have been having fun. I wasn't sure how well this worked until the next time we were in this situation and all the water went in the pool instead of up in the air.

We let the child assign the colours to different feelings. The colour the child then selects for people's speech shows us how he perceived that person's emotion. This can alert us to misperceptions of other people's emotions and prompt a discussion.

## Blue people

Blue is the favourite colour in marketing. It's a colour that evokes positive feelings and trust. Using shades of blue for people allows us to begin to explain social relationships and behaviour that may not be obvious to young people with autism.

Tony Attwood is a British psychologist who now lives in Queensland, Australia. He has had numerous books published on Asperger's Syndrome, including the acclaimed Complete Guide to Asperger's Syndrome which is widely regarded as the definitive guide to Asperger's Syndrome. He is an entertaining and insightful speaker, with a busy schedule of international workshops. I attended a workshop in April 2013. He loves the company of people with autism and can see from their perspective. Instinct, love and truth have combined to make him an outstanding psychologist. Attwood shares the strategies and practical tools he has developed in order to set more young people with Asperger's Syndrome on a path to success.

Tony Attwood devised an effective way to explain relationships and social behaviour to the visual learner. He suggests taking a big piece of paper and drawing a series of concentric circles with the student at the centre. His immediate family members are closest, followed by other close family and friends. As we add other people to the outer circles, we can explain social interactions visually.

> A handshake may be an appropriate greeting for the doctor but not the expected greeting for a grandma. The child may really like and admire his/her teachers but greeting them with a hug and kiss each morning would not be an age-appropriate thing for a seven-year-old to do. An alternative affectionate but verbal greeting can be suggested. (Attwood 2007, p.76)

It can be helpful to add colours or numbers to the circles so they can be quickly referenced. Using shades of blue can work well, with pale blue at the centre getting darker and graduating to navy blue for the outer circle. This way you can quickly reference a person with an associated number or colour, which gives an immediate visual reminder without social awkwardness.

By adding a gradient of light blue to dark blue we add a visual to refer to. You could say that person would be dark blue (meaning they are a stranger). The student might connect with previous social learning about 'dark blue people'. (Do not use a gradient that goes from blue to black because this could set the student on the path towards another misconnection.)

*Figure 6.3 Blue social context symbol*

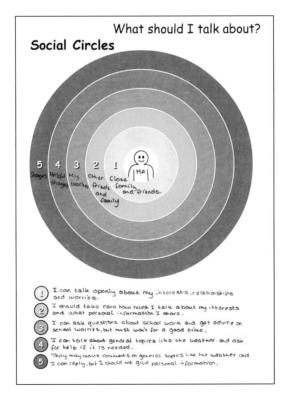

*Figure 6.4 Blue social circles visual*

Mounting visuals of one-to-one staff on blue card as in Figure 6.5 shows that they are 'people who help' and are not strangers to the child.

*Figure 6.5 One-to-one support staff photos added to the schedule*

If a child is on a one-to-one programme, it may reduce anxiety knowing which staff will be working with him. Adding photos of people to the 'now' and 'next' visual tells children who will be there to help them. Surrounding the photos with a mid-blue background also sends the message that these are people who help us, but not immediate family. If children have attachment issues, they may find it reassuring to see who will be working with them. It can also help highlight if they have a preference for who works with them. We can use this information and link favoured staff with the children when planning activities we know they might find more challenging. We must never let children get used to having their favoured member of staff all the time or we set them up to fail when that staff member is off sick or changes role.

Using blue for people also links well with the blue colour-coded symbol the child uses to ask for 'help'. Colour coding people helps the child create another group. This might make people seem less confusing and help the child to decode social situations. As Naoki Higashida explains, 'Invisible things like human relationships and ambiguous expressions, however, these are difficult for us people with autism to get our heads around' (Higashida 2013, p.113).

## Measuring emotions

Tony Attwood suggests that an individual with Asperger's Syndrome might be 'more able to quantify an emotional response accurately using a numerical representation of the graduation in experience and expression of emotions rather than a precise and subtle vocabulary of words'. He suggests using an 'emotion thermometer, bar graph or volume scale' (Attwood 2007, p.135).

### The Incredible 5-Point Scale

*The Incredible 5-Point Scale* was developed by autism resource specialists Kari Dunn Buron and Mitzi Beth Curtis (2003). The scale gives a visual structure to describe anxiety on a scale. It can also be used to help children self-manage their behaviour. They learn the number that links with how they feel and what they should do in that situation. The colours add a visual code to those numbers.

*Figure 6.6 A child was able to scale noises and show that a kettle boiling was awful whereas fireworks were okay*

Be careful about showing faces attached to numbers and colours. If children have no understanding of using the scale they could look at the expression, the number and the colour and make their own connection. We do not want them to think that red fives always represent anger, because the scale can be used to scale grief, worry or discomfort.

## *The emotions colour wheel*

Using an emotions colour wheel can be a good way to explain how emotions graduate and have many layers. The children can learn the language for explaining the severity of the emotion. They might feel angry, but are they 'upset' or totally 'enraged'?

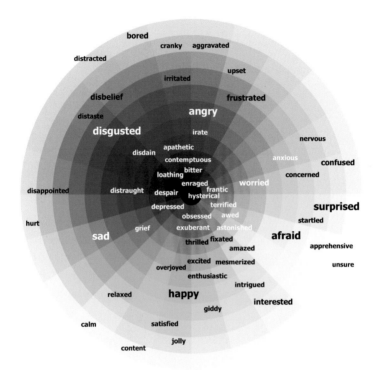

The Emotions Color Wheel can help visually group feelings. Click on a feeling in the color wheel to learn more about it.

*Figure 6.7 The emotions colour wheel*

The website www.do2learn.com has an emotions colour wheel which is free to use. Click an emotion and more information is shown. There is a photo of someone showing the emotion and an explanation.

## Outsmarting explosive behaviour

The autistic artist and author Judy Endow developed a visual system to help her son (who also has autism) outsmart his explosive behaviour. She has since published the idea and used it to help other children. Using something that motivates the child, the system shows the stages of behaviour and provides a series of strategies to stop the explosion *en route* before it happens. She used coloured train carriages to illustrate the stages of escalation. Red 'stop' and green 'go' signs show positive behavioural supports that might help avoid the behaviour escalating. Endow states that escalating behaviour has four distinct phases and the best way to avoid 'the crash' is to stop the behaviour before it picks up steam. She explains that there is a point of no return when we know the explosion will happen. At this stage the best thing to do is try to create a safe environment. We look around for any objects that could be used to cause harm and clear the room of other children who might get hurt. During the explosion we contain and we then restore and 'restore the track'. Endow states that this system has been used to help many young people with autism manage their behaviour (Endow 2009).

There are many strategies and supports that feature again and again for individuals with autism – a good night's sleep, a full stomach, structure, a calm environment and a clear plan. We cannot risk a child arriving in an educational setting and going straight to the fight/flight point of no return. Any known supports should be set up ready and we should ensure that the child's first impressions make him feel secure and happy.

It is vital we teach children with autism to regulate 'explosive behaviour', because society will not tolerate individuals who could harm others. Autistic adults who cannot control these behaviours become a danger and this will impact on their freedom in society.

These strategies and supports are like tools. We start off with a basic set and as our experience builds so does our tool kit. In time we learn to use specific tools for certain situations. We know that the faster we can get our hand on the precise tool, the more perfect the results. But we all start out with the basic tool kit.

When teaching children with autism, we draw on strategies we have in our kit and use what we think will work. We may use visuals, scales and Social Stories™. All of these strategies were once new. They were invented by physiologists, teachers, parents or adults with autism and were born out of need. We must never disregard an idea because it is not what *we* are used to. We must constantly invent and not be afraid to trial ideas. The more we tailor our tools to individuals, decode social situations and explain emotions, the better outcomes we will see.

Architects mix mathematical certainty with invention to create their plans. They need a team to make their plan a reality. Builders use every tool at their disposal to make the architect's vision a reality. If the right tool does not exist, the builder may also become an inventor. The more heart and soul that goes into the building from everyone involved, the better it will be.

The educator has a plan. Like the architect, she will need a team assisting and willing to believe in the plan. Everyone involved must be ready to adapt, rethink and invent. The architect and the educator know the importance of foundations and supports. They want their structures to serve humanity beyond their lifetimes. The architect plans brilliant buildings and interior designers then decorate them. The educator digs foundations and structures supports, hoping that in the future the child will add his own design and colour.

# Chapter 7

# Sporting Colours

'If a man does not keep pace with his companions, perhaps it is because he hears a *different* drummer. Let him step to the music which he hears, however measured or far away.'

Henry David Thoreau

Next on the schedule is PE. We walk down the corridor into a small enclosed room. It's too small – not like the classroom. The room echoes loudly and smells disgusting. Now I'm given a bag of clothes. They are expecting me to take my clothes off! I *never* take my clothes of in the middle of the day. Why would I change my clothes? I curl into a ball refusing. The other children change their clothes and leave. Every so often a teacher shows me the bag of clothes and a PE symbol. No way! She will not let me leave the small, smelly room until the other children return full of noise. The teacher is sad because I did not change my clothes. I was not expecting to. I hate PE.

This account is fictional, not a case study, but it illustrates the point that the changing room can be a huge barrier for some children with autism. Because they cannot get past the horror of the changing room, they miss out on sport.

I asked Scott James (the singer with Asperger's Syndrome who found fame though *The X Factor*) about his experience of sport at school. He recalled:

PE in school wasn't much fun for me. I lacked the ability to socialise properly with my peers, and the changing rooms were small and packed, which didn't do much for my senses. My co-ordination for sport was sorely lacking and playing anything that involved a ball or tracking anything was often a big ask.

I was always picked last, made fun of, and usually the one with the least amount of aptitude in any physical ability. In school I was somewhat on the larger side, which certainly didn't help matters, either with the other students or in terms of general mobility across our playing field.

Unfortunately this lasted through most of my school life, before my school finally began to understand that PE wasn't really for me, and offered to help me in other ways. (Scott James, personal communication, 2013)

So what can we do to improve the first experience of sport at school? First, I think we need to look at the timetable. Teachers often use the 'PE' symbol and miss out the 'changing'. To us changing might be a natural part of the session, but to the child with autism it may be a totally alien idea. You could let the class do the first PE session in their school uniform so they can learn what PE is like before the changing room hurdle. Make the first lesson really fun and not too challenging. If you have equipment for sensory integration, such as a trampoline or a big bouncy ball, get these out.

When we introduce any sport to children with autism, we must set it up so that they can succeed at their comfort level. Structure the activities so that the expectation is very clear. Encourage, cajole, model, but never *make* children do something that frightens them. To us, walking along the balance beam may seem like a small request, but we do not know how a child sees it. If possible, group the child with others who have a similar ability level. Do not send a child onto a tennis court if he does not yet have the co-ordination to *catch* a ball. Build the child's trust and make the experience of sport fun. Use lots of rewards and praise. Sport must not be associated with fear or discomfort. Once children see they can do something, they will want to challenge themselves to do more.

When you first visit the field with the children, do so on a day when the weather conditions are good. It cannot be raining as this may upset their senses. It cannot be too sunny because the brightness may hurt their eyes. If they begin with a positive experience, they are more likely to go again. If PE is sometimes in the hall and sometimes on the field, show them where it will be with a picture. Have a different transition board for each, if the children use them.

Try to get as much bounce or physical energy release as possible out of the children so they get quite hot. Follow the PE lesson with a lesson looking at different sports. Look at some video clips. Make a note if any of the children show interest in a particular sport. This could be helpful information later on. This lesson will have laid some groundwork for an activity in the style of Carol Gray's Social Stories™ (Gray 2000) should any sport-related issues arise later. What do the children notice about the sports people? Let the children focus on what the players are wearing. Why do people change their clothes to do sports? If possible, visit a sports centre where the children can see other people doing sports. After all this social learning, ask for their opinions. Is school uniform a good thing to wear for PE? Why not? Try to get the children to come up with the idea that they could change for PE. Often the child with autism will be happy to do something if the reason is explained. Whereas other children might accept changing as a routine with little explanation, the autistic child likes to know our reasons. We must respect this need to question and offer visual explanations. These children will not follow directions blindly. Neither did Einstein, Newton or Mozart. Original thinkers will always question, and we must nurture these enquiring minds.

## The changing room

Explain that next time you are going to change for PE because you think you would do better in sports clothes. The children might like to change too. Introducing it like this means they still have an option not to change. Not changing does not mean that they do not do PE. If changing is part of the PE lesson, it should be included on the class timetable. Each changing room slot should be linked with a ten-minute timer. The PE symbol is sandwiched between them and shows the length of the session. This way, you start out on the right foot. The children know what you have planned and how long it will last. You will not have ruined the picture they had of their day. Maybe they still won't get changed, but at least they still trust their teacher and don't miss the whole lesson.

When you go to the changing rooms, take the timer that links with the timetable so the children can see the time elapse. When the timer is finished, you leave the changing room – whether the children have changed or not. This way they still get to do PE and still experience the changing room. In time they may decide to get changed. Always take their clothes, just in case, and suggest they change, but never react to them not changing.

*Figure 7.1 The PE symbol between two changing room symbols with timers*

Stopping a child from doing PE is not the answer. I've seen children spend the whole PE session sat outside the changing room. They refuse to go into the changing room so they don't do PE, but what does this achieve?

Use the personal care schedules to show the stages of getting undressed and dressed. Let the child see another child go through the stages with the visual schedule. When he has changed, give lots of praise. It is hoped that this will have taken less than the ten minutes and because of this he can leave sooner. It is hoped that your reluctant changer will notice this.

If changing continues to be an issue, it might be worth calling home to see if on PE day you could find a compromise on uniform. Sometimes we have to take small steps. Not changing for PE is more likely to be because of anxiety, perception or habit than behaviour.

Wearing a helmet for riding a bike or a horse is non-negotiable because it is for the child's safety. This does mean that some children will not be able to access these activities and they may not understand, but their safety is the priority. The stick people on the riding and bike timetable symbols must show people wearing helmets to avoid confusion. Again, we can use the internet to look at pictures of professional jockeys and cyclists so the child sees helmets being used outside school.

*Figure 7.2 A 'getting dressed' schedule*

## Go green for action and sport!

Our sport schedules and symbols have a green colour code. The green relates to the traffic light 'Go!' PE symbols can be printed as squares (shown in Figure 7.3) or circles. The circular shape again relates to the 'Go!', but also to balls (found in all PE cupboards).

We use visuals showing activities and actions in PE lessons. A green colour code immediately tells children with autism to file this in their 'get active' drawer. As they learn different skills, they can build their knowledge bank. They might recall how when they first encountered a balance beam they were frightened, but they overcame this. Use the PE symbols to remind children of these past achievements. Remind them what they can do, using the green symbols so that they make a connection.

*Figure 7.3 Green 'getting active' symbols*

Children might not need the visual to explain what they need to do in PE. They might be capable of simply copying the activity. And we do not always have to use symbols – we use what is appropriate for the child – so, for example, a handwritten written 'jump' sign may be enough. However, the colour code is still useful because it tells children that this activity is part of the active things and helps them to generalise all the different sporting activities. We often use the encouraging comment 'It's like learning to ride a bike.' This comment makes no sense to the literal thinker, but linking it with the colour green does make sense. One day, when they are struggling with a 'green' activity such as riding a bike, they will remember all the green things they *can* do. This will raise their self-esteem, create a more positive attitude and, it is hoped, alleviate some anxiety.

## PE lessons

When the green symbols are on display, there is a good visual indication that the lesson is going to be PE. This is useful if the room for PE is multi-purpose. Often the school hall is also used for singing, plays and assemblies, when expectations are quite different.

As well as colour coding the activities, you can add a colour code to the changing room door if you have a set changing room for PE. PE bags or boxes could be colour coded green as another visual link.

Colour can add structure to PE lessons. You can colour code activity areas using tape or hoops. You could label areas with a corresponding coloured card. Children could use a quick visual tick list or postbox to mark off activities as they go.

Sometimes we want the children to try everything, but this might not come naturally. If they like climbing the wall bars, why should they move on? If they have to collect a tick or a sticker of each colour during the lesson, they will be more likely to try new apparatus. Tick charts and stickers are little motivators and rewards that a lot of children respond to. There could also be a reward for getting all their ticks or stickers.

*Figure 7.4 Using colour codes in PE*

## Order in the PE cupboard

There is a good reason for using colour coding to organise a cupboard. Even when people can read labels, often they do not take the time to read them. However, if, for example, you have a red bucket, a blue bucket and small red balls and large blue balls, the children (and busy staff) are more likely to put everything back in its proper place.

## Mapping success through colour

Colour can also show the measure of success in sport. Think of horse show rosettes, swimming badges and karate belts. Moving on to a new colour is often used to show progress in sport. The colour system was put in place because it motivates.

Creating your own colour-coded reward system might raise self-esteem and keep children motivated before they are ready to try for a badge. This helps to illustrate that we cannot do things perfectly straightaway. For example, a child learning to ride a bike could be given a red sticker for the first time he puts a helmet on, a purple sticker the first time he goes on a balance bike, a blue sticker for learning to balance on the bike and a green sticker when he is able to ride a two-wheeled bike. Colour codes show the child that learning is done in stages and that nobody gets on a bike and is able to ride it straightaway.

*Figure 7.5 A child learning to ride a bike in stages*

Another visual way to show that achieving in PE is gradual is to use rainbows. The rainbow stickers can be used in lessons and then each time the child achieves a step you can colour in a layer of a rainbow. These can go in the child's progress file or be displayed on the wall. It's a lovely way to show a child what can be achieved if he keeps on trying.

If you can, add photos of the child at Stage 1 (starting out and trying) and Stage 7 (achieving the end goal), as illustrated in Figure 7.6. The 'can do' rainbow in Figure 7.6 was made independently by a child who had just learnt to ride a two wheel bike. She understood about the different stages and decided that she'd been through those seven stages while learning to ride her bike. Seeing this child take off on a two wheel bike, having found a way to conquer something I had never mastered, was incredible. She had achieved so much in such a short time, turning a 'can't' into a definite 'can'.

Filed together, a child's 'wow' achievements are great for building a collection of positive images that will boost self-esteem and remind him what he can do.

If we can help children find a sport they enjoy, they may find something they can do with their free time when they finish education. Continuing with sport will help their physical health. Obesity is a reality and we need to encourage all children to exercise to counteract this. Adults with autism often spend far too long sat at the computer. If they develop an interest in sport during childhood, they are more likely to continue to exercise and this could protect not only their physical but emotional well-being in the future. The sad reality is that adults with autism can be prone to depression, obesity, anxiety and addiction. This may impact on the friendships they develop and the way that they spend their free time. Exercise can raise self-esteem and provide a healthy way of releasing energy and relaxing.

*Figure 7.6 An 'I can' resource for riding a bike (the child can look back at this and recall overcoming a hurdle)*

# Chapter 8

# **Colour Codes in Lessons**
## *Literacy, Numeracy, Science, ICT and Geography*

'We build too many walls and not enough bridges.'

Isaac Newton

Colour codes can help teach children tricky concepts and introduce new ideas in a familiar way. Colours can provide a visual structure and build independence. We use the colours as scaffolds within our lessons, aware that in time they may not be required.

## Literacy
### *'Colourful Semantics'*

In 1997, speech and language therapist (SLT) Alison Bryan (Bryan 1997) published details of a new therapy called 'Colourful Semantics'. She used colour codes to break down sentence structures.

When introducing language we can establish things by pointing and using pictures, photographs and symbols. 'Colourful Semantics' helps teach those less concrete parts of a sentence – the 'whats' and the 'wheres'.

'Colourful Semantics' introduces grammar without teaching it. Using the colour codes motivates and speeds learning. The children learn by matching the colours. In time they are able to categorise and order words without the colours.

The colours and format of 'Colourful Semantics' are:

- 'who' (the subject) – orange

- 'doing what' (the verb) – yellow

- 'to what' (the object) – green

- 'where' (location) – blue.

Sarah Davis is a practising speech therapist who founded Integrated Treatment Services in 2006 following a successful partnership in Independent therapy and a long standing history within the NHS.

> When I worked in a speech and language unit in Leicestershire, we had children who were unable to write a sentence, let alone half a page. With the use of 'Colourful Semantics', we encouraged children to make coloured picture strips to describe a book they had just read as a class, or to describe an activity they had just done. Initially the children would just stick in the coloured pictures in order to record their ideas. They would soon begin to copy the key words from the pictures and gradually they would begin to write in the little words, such as 'the', 'and', 'under the'. Before long the children were able to write sentences on their own, using the 'Colourful Semantics' as just a prompt. Colourful Semantics can really scaffold emerging literacy skills and help the child gain confidence really quickly. (Davis 2008)

I contacted Chris Wade, Director of London Speech and Language Therapists, who was working closely with Alison Bryan in making a new 'Colourful Semantics' app. Chris confirmed that there is no significance to the colours themselves in the 'Colourful Semantics' theory. As with our colour codes, consistency is the important thing here. The 'Colourful Semantics' app has been developed by Therapy Box and will include a feature where you can change the colours. The colours are there to create a visual link and a structure.

A child who can read should not use the symbols. Take colour-coded pens and encourage the child to underline subject, verb, object and location. Children pick up on this fast. Using the colours to break down language makes more sense than using more words to describe.

*Figure 8.1 'Colourful Semantics'*

## Shape coding and 'Colourful Semantics'

Susan Ebbels worked as an SLT at Moor House School in Surrey, where they were already using 'Colourful Semantics'. By incorporating some of the principles of 'Colourful Semantics', she developed a coding scheme using shapes which enables not just thematic role information but complex syntactic information to be coded and manipulated. Alison Bryan has worked in collaboration with Susan Ebbels and incorporated 'Shape Coding' so it can be used as a progression from 'Colourful Semantics'. Ebbels (2007, p.70) gives these examples:

- noun phrase 'the BOY' – oval

- verb phrase 'THROWS the ball' – hexagon

- prepositional phrase 'IN the box' – semicircle

- adjective phrase 'BIGGER than a cat' – cloud.

*Figure 8.2 Sorting nouns, verbs and adjectives into coloured pots*

I am not suggesting the child always writes using these colours, but they can be a good visual way to teach the initial concepts of grammar.

- Give the child three pots and a selection of nouns, verbs and adjectives written in a corresponding colour.

- If you have been using 'Colourful Semantics', I suggest you follow the same colours to avoid confusion.

# Numeracy
## *Using Numicon*

*Figure 8.3 Numicon*

Numicon is a hands-on practical resource which allows children to physically explore the relationships between numbers. The colours and shapes will instantly appeal. Temple Grandin suggests that we:

> Use concrete visual methods to teach number concepts. My parents gave me a math toy which helped me to learn numbers. It consisted of a set of blocks which had a different length and a different colour for the numbers one through ten. With this I learned how to add and subtract. (Grandin 2002)

Numicon comes with coloured 'connectors' so that children can develop understanding of number relationships by building. The connectors being coloured could be distracting to the visual learner. Look at Figure 8.4 – this has no order and could confuse and bother a visual learner.

*Figure 8.4 Numicon with coloured connectors*

Numicon sell sets of black and white connectors, which I would recommend for learners with autism. By using black or white connectors, we remove the potential distraction.

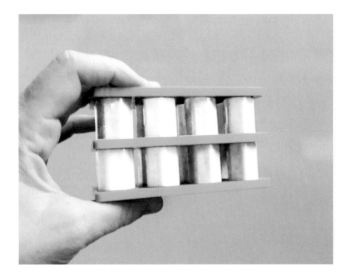

*Figure 8.5 Numicon with white connectors may be less*
*visually distracting for learners with autism*

Children with autism will, like Grandin, make sense of the colours and connect with them, which will motivate them to learn.

Numicon is not only coloured but weighted, so the children can feel the difference between numbers. If they use scales, they can begin to grasp concepts such as equals seeing that four balance against two and two. Our five-year-old son's teacher is a big fan of their new Numicon resource and couldn't believe how fast her class took to naming numbers. The children use the Numicon in art with playdough. All the time the children are playing, they are exploring numbers.

There is also Numicon software to extend learning further and a wealth of ideas available through the site and from teachers who blog to share good practice. I think this would be a fantastic resource for children with autism to have access to in a nursery setting. It might even be a good way to get them playing alongside other children.

## Floor spots

Floor spots can help children learn to line up and keep to their own personal space, but they can also be used to teach about different things. I change floor spots each half term, linking them with changing topics. We've had different colours, coins, shapes, colours, sea creatures and buildings. Keeping visuals fresh increases the children's interest.

The 2D shape floor spots are also included on the CD-ROM and can be used to structure lining up, but I would not introduce them until you are certain of consistent understanding of colour language. Unfamiliar colour names linked with the more complicated shapes could be too much learning and result in confusions such as calling the hexagon an indigo (not what we are after).

Start with the colour floor spots. Only once *all* children know the colour names, should the shapes be used.

We often link our floor spots with our topic. If we are learning about money, we have coins or purses. If it's time, we have clocks showing different times. This way, the children are learning each time they line up.

## Why we should not colour numbers

While I think colours do help explain many concepts, I would be cautious about colouring individual numbers or letters because it might contradict the way a child already colour codes and cause confusion. The most common form of synaesthesia is seeing numbers or letters as colours. Where autism and synaesthesia co-exist, colouring numbers could cause confusion and hinder learning. Through my research I have found that synaesthesia and autism co-exist often enough that I would avoid colouring numbers and letters just in case.

*Figure 8.6 Making sense of number bonds using colour*

There are many other ways we can bring colour into our numeracy lessons. The child in the photograph above is learning number bonds to ten. There are two different colours of plastic animals in the box. The children each take ten and write a number sentence to match how many they have of each colour. Instant structure!

*Figure 8.7 Coloured resources to teach fractions, percentages and decimals*

Figure 8.7 shows how colours can help children understand fractions and link them with percentages and decimals. The colours explain the concept really quickly.

These are helpful visuals for every child, but can dramatically alter the odds of understanding for a young person with autism. Add a colour code and suddenly a tricky concept such as fractions has a visual explanation.

Children may create their own colour systems for learning – let them develop these. Jake Barnett's mother recalls him creating a visual based language:

> This language uses colours and shapes to represent numbers and combinations of them to represent equations. Imagine an Abacus colliding with a kaleidoscope and you're close. He layers transparencies in different colours on top of a light box now, but back then he had thousands of pieces of construction paper, meticulously cut into shapes that could be laid on top of one another so that he could do complex calculations. (Barnett 2013a, pp.119–120)

## Science

What do we do in science? We find answers. We experiment. We learn magic. If only I'd had a science teacher who had told me we were learning the secrets behind magic, my attitude would have been so different.

*Figure 8.8 Coloured science resources*

Coloured equipment and instructions within a science lesson can help pupils carry out experiments independently.

Demonstrate first, then give equipment to a member of support staff so that she can model the correct process for the children.

We know that children with autism are naturally keen to investigate, explore and test. Let them get hands-on in science lessons and, if it is safe, allow them to experiment. You never know what they might be exploring or what they might come up with in the future.

### Colourful science

There are many ways you use colour to demonstrate scientific facts:

- Growing things: Add a gardening symbol to the timetable. Watering plants can be a lovely way to end the school day.

- Osmosis: Put white, cut flowers into water with different coloured dyes and watch them change colour. This demonstrates osmosis and attracts the child's attention.

- Sinking and floating: Add blue food colouring to water and freeze. Set the frozen ice boats to sail in water.

- Light and dark: Make a sensory light tunnel using a box lined with a piece of silver safety blanket and a colour-changing light.

## ICT
### Colour-coded software

When we first developed our SEN Assist Fairy Tales software, I knew that the first level had to be fast and achievable. By using colour codes on certain questions, we gave children a familiar visual cue. For example, in the pronouns section the 'male' and 'female' pictures are outlined in blue and pink, creating a visual link with the colours around the answers 'he' and 'she'. When students are given this code to follow, they get it right and learn to complete the set of activities independently. Children with autism do not like getting it wrong and we don't want them always seeking a prompt. As they move on to level two, the colour code is removed, but the concept of 'he' and 'she' has often started to sink in because of the visual connections.

Autistic children don't just use colour codes to match. They enjoy trying to discover the connections.

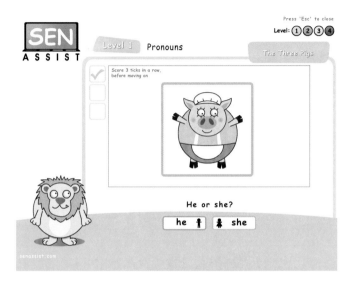

*Figure 8.9 Colour codes in SEN Assist software*

## Colour-coded hardware

There is a lot of colour-coded computer hardware available. You may like to try some of the following ideas:

- Coloured keyboards may help children who are learning to type by breaking the keyboard down into smaller areas of focus.

- In the past I have taken photographs and made large keyboards to teach children where the letters of their name are by matching them.

- You could also make the child's computer login his name so that he has a purpose in typing it.

You can see how the keyboard in Figure 8.10 will also be a good visual reference when you are teaching about vowels. 'The vowels are the purple letters on our keyboard' gives students an immediate visual link.

*Figure 8.10 A colour-coded keyboard*

Having a colour-coded mouse like the one in Figure 8.11 can help children learn about the left and right click much faster.

*Figure 8.11 The frog sticker on this computer mouse shows the child where to click*

## Geography

Geography is a subject that comes fully colour coded. How do we distinguish the sea and land on the map? Countries are colour coded, as are street maps, weather systems and recycling bins. Look to geography as an example. The colour coding is already in place.

*Figure 8.12 Colours used on a map*

*Figure 8.13 Colour-coded recycling bins*

# Chapter 9

# Colours to Encourage Creativity
## Cooking, Gardening, Music, Sensory and Art

'I know that these broken pieces, arranged just so,
with the right bonding, can come together once
again to become a uniquely beautiful mosaic.'

Maribel Danta

## Cooking

Children with autism often love cooking. It's practical, visual, sensory and can raise self-esteem. Daniel Tammet says he cooks 'regularly because it is a tactile experience that helps me relax' (Tammet 2007, p.274). Children often seem more relaxed and focused in cooking lessons. I think they enjoy the structure and can see a clear point to the activity.

Cooking lessons are not just about making cakes. They allow us to incorporate and assess so many other skills. Cooking is an opportunity for:

- learning

- sharing

- waiting

- communicating

- measuring

- counting

- fractions

- following instructions

- working independently

- co-operating

- listening

- experiencing food.

*Figure 9.1 Cooking using colour-coded equipment*

We can use these sessions to teach about safety (the oven is hot and can be dangerous), to ask for help and to build tolerance for trying new foods. The more children handle food and are involved in food preparation, the more normal the idea of trying new foods seems. When I bring our warm bread or pizzas from the oven, the classroom is filled with the delicious, sensory smell. The children then wait for it to cool enough for them to try whatever they have cooked. There is no pressure, but we have made great leaps forward with some of our fussier eaters.

Bread might sound tricky, but it's one of the best recipes to start with and you can always cheat a little by buying bread mix. There are many reasons I think bread is a good starting point. Over the years I have seen so many lunchboxes belonging to children with autism that contain plain bread rolls instead of sandwiches or other savoury foods. They seem to be a common starting point when a child has issues with food. I start cooking with plain bread rolls because then the lesson has a purpose to the child with a limited diet. We are making something they might eat. If I can get a child to try a plain bread roll one week I might get away with adding cheese the following week. Then there is the sensory element of kneading the warm dough, and the bread smells amazing when it's cooked. The aroma wafts around the corridors and the children hear so many positive comments about the school's budding young chefs. Let the children try the bread while it's still warm and perhaps add a social element by encouraging them to share their cooking with other people. Seeing the results of their efforts and receiving a lot of praise from you and others can really raise their self-esteem.

*Figure 9.2 Cheese and onion bread rolls made by a class of children with autism using colour-coded equipment*

As the term goes on, add ingredients. You can keep making bread each week for half a term. Try sun-dried tomato bread, pizza, cheese and onion rolls and wholemeal plaits. With each passing week, the children will become more independent.

*Figure 9.3 A child using colour codes for cooking*

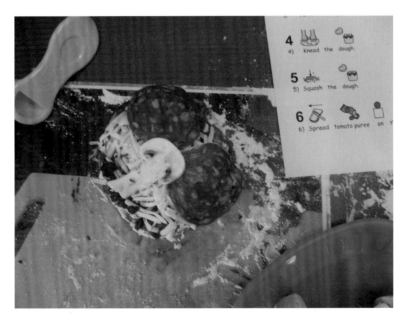

*Figure 9.4 A pizza face made by a child following a*
*visual recipe and using colour-coded equipment*

Encourage creativity in these sessions. So long as the children follow the recipe, why shouldn't they make a funny face or flower on their pizza. When you model making things, show the creative thought process. Pause to think where you want to put things. Let your cooking planning evolve and get the children's suggestions for recipes. These sessions will have even greater appeal when they see cooking as inventive, experimental and creative.

By colour coding the bowls, measures and utensils, the 'method' or instructions can be made even more visual. Figure 9.3 shows children cooking using colour-coded equipment. I particularly like the way the measuring cups are shaped to show a full cup, half a cup and a quarter cup. Using colour-coded equipment they can measure quantities before they can read numbers or distinguish the difference between a teaspoon and tablespoon. We can show on the recipe that they should use the red tablespoon. In time they will learn the different sizes and measures.

If you have access to a symbols programme, you can insert photos that relate directly to the equipment you are using, which will also help the children learn to follow the recipe independently.

Children learn to take ownership by following colour-coded instructions. They achieve independence faster as the colour adds structure. Children become more independent and select what they need. Encourage children to ask others to pass them things. As well as learning cooking skills, they can also learn turn-taking, co-operation and waiting skills.

*Figure 9.5 Colour-coded cooking equipment*

Being able to follow a recipe builds self-esteem and independence – so important for young people with autism!

Ideally, each child needs his own set of equipment. After cooking sessions at school our washing-up looks like we have fed the 5,000. We have, in fact, made nine very 'individual' fish cakes, bread rolls or biscuits.

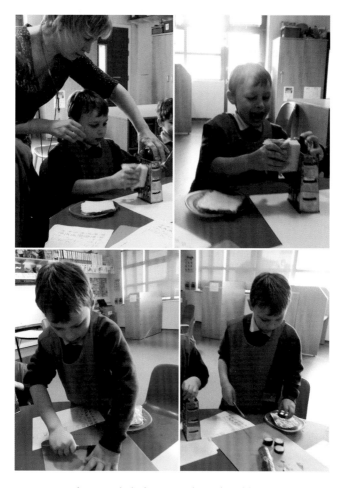

*Figure 9.6 Colour-coded chopping boards add interest as well as teaching children about cross-contamination of surfaces*

Colour-coded chopping boards alleviate the risk of bacterial cross-contamination. They started out being used in professional kitchens, but are now used in many homes. They are a quick, visual way of consistently having separate boards for raw meat, raw fish, cooked meat, salad and fruit, vegetables and dairy. In a busy kitchen, colour speaks faster than words.

*Figure 9.7 Children learn to stack and put away equipment by using colour*
This stack from Joseph Joseph includes a sieve, colander, bowls and measuring cups.

A young person can learn to stack these bowls. It is a functional task with a clear purpose. Learning to put things away is a very important life skill. If we can create a natural instinct to tidy up, we will set children up to have a tidier home and more ordered workplace. Colour codes are used in professional kitchens because they are a quick, multilinguistic visual, and by teaching the children to follow them, we could be introducing an important skill, which could lead to future employment.

## Case study

Lenny was seven years old and his limited diet was beginning to cause concern. He would refuse to eat anything at snack time other than cornflakes.

He would try to eat non-food substances such as playdough and glue. In art lessons he would be so quick at grabbing the glue, our reactions had to be fast.

We started our cooking sessions by making individual biscuits. Lenny enjoyed the sensory aspect of these sessions and would have a cheeky taste of the mixture afterwards. Next, we moved on to cup cakes. Again, the mixture was sweet and tempting.

Following this, we started making bread rolls. We began with simple white bread rolls, moving on to adding ingredients such as cheese and sun-dried tomatoes. The smell of freshly baked bread wafted down the corridor and Lenny began to eat the bread, including additions of cheese, sun-dried tomatoes and onion. Pizza was next. One of my best teacher moments was seeing Lenny devour a pepperoni pizza.

When we started our 'Under the Sea' topic, I wondered what Lenny would make of our salmon fishcakes. I was delighted to see him try the smoked salmon and then happily eat his whole fishcake. Through cooking he was soon eating spinach, sweetcorn, nutmeg, potato, egg, smoked salmon and even prawns. All these healthy foods he previously would not touch were suddenly okay.

This was not limited to school either. At weekends Lenny cooked with his family. He was gaining so many practical skills, but he was eating a growing variety of foods which would lead him to have a healthier balanced diet and could subsequently improve his health as an adult.

## Gardening

Gardening, like cooking, is a hands-on lesson. I've included gardening because people with autism often have a love of nature. Also, it's sensory, satisfying, easy to structure and has a clear point. 'Gardening provides good exercise and is relaxing, requires patience and dedication and helps me feel a greater connection with the world around me' (Tammet 2007, p.275).

The following tips can help to make gardening lessons successful:

- Colour code the equipment and use visual instructions.

- Start with something simple, such as growing cress. When the cress has grown, you can use it in a cooking lesson. The children will get great satisfaction from making egg and cress sandwiches with cress they have grown.

- Beans are another satisfying plant because they grow tall fast. Always plant a few extras. The children will not like it if their beans do not grow.

- Sometimes digging can help children feel more relaxed because they have something hands-on to do.

## Music

Colour codes can give children a shortcut to learning to play an instrument. This is not only for children on the spectrum, but offers a motivating starting point for all children. There are books available and instruments pre-labelled or strung with colour-coded strings. I prefer systems where the music is still drawn out correctly but notes are coloured to correspond to the keys, holes or strings. This way the child sees sense in the notes and could potentially learn to read them without colours.

*Figure 9.8 Colour-coded notes in the 'Rainbow Colours' ukulele book*

*Figure 9.9 Learning to play the ukulele with colour-coded strings*

'Rainbow Colours' produce colour-coded guitars and ukuleles along with books. I'm not convinced that I, as a non-musician, could begin to teach ukulele or guitar without video tutorials, but we already have success using colour codes to teach children to play the keyboard.

The 'Rainbow Piano Technique' was developed by a mother trying to teach her son to play the piano. The child learns to play by pressing the correct colour keys. Once the child is able to play and follow the music, the necessity to use colours should fade so that he can play a piano without the colour code.

*Figure 9.10 Learning to play the keyboard with colour-coded keys*

Colour codes can be added to most lessons and help a learner with autism learn because they increase the chances of quick success. The child follows the colours and in time learns to complete activities without them.

## Art

Colour can be used in many ways to motivate and add structure to art sessions. Art activities must be something all the children can do independently. The teacher creates a model of the end result and children then select the materials for their individual creations. Ideally, a member of support staff will be able to work on a project alongside some of the children. This way the support staff can model asking for and getting things.

To encourage creativity it is important to have a variety of materials available. Some students will try to copy exactly what you made. This is fine, but there may be artists in the group who, given the freedom of selection, can come up with something really creative. We must not quash individual creativity in our art lessons. These are lessons when each child should be given the chance to explore his own imagination.

## Silk painting

Silk painting is a lovely activity that can really appeal to those who like perfection but struggle with colouring, because the gutta stops paint spreading beyond the lines. For some children I prepare the silk screen with lines drawn so they can simply fill in the colours. Other children are able to draw pictures themselves. The children often love to see the way the silk paints spread and then stop at the lines of gutta.

I recall doing a lesson with a 'rainbow fish' theme. I showed the children what to do and gave them the paints and gutta. They were all totally involved and engaged, but not everyone had followed the 'rainbow fish' theme. One had done a detailed Dalek from *Dr Who* and another produced an incredible multicoloured robot. I think these children expected me to try to stop them going off plan, but in art I think it's important to let them get carried away with their creativity. I'm certain the robot was a much better creation than a forced 'rainbow fish' would have been. Sometimes we must let these children go their own creative way. They should be allowed to base their art on what they love.

## Junk modelling

There's something really satisfying about turning a cardboard box into a toy. To fit in with our buildings topic, each child designed a room in the house. This meant the art was individual but followed a theme. The children really enjoyed choosing flooring, wallpaper and tiles. They chose pictures of their motivators for the walls. When finished, we put all the boxes together to form a house. The children cut out little figures to go inside and had a lovely time playing with their model house.

Another time our topic was the farm. I happened to have nine identical boxes I'd hung onto after we bought our colour-coded cooking equipment. Each child created his own individual model farm. The children loved painting the grass, adding enclosures and shelters. They were then totally engaged in their play with our plastic animals, sorting them into their areas, adding a new fence, a sign and some straw.

It's so important to show these children what fun they can have from creating their own toys before they discover computer games.

## Collage

Collage is a great way to encourage creativity. The child can choose pictures and materials. Each child could have a colour as his theme. Let the children choose a piece of coloured paper, then draw a big bubble word of their chosen colour. The children then find things of that colour to stick to their paper. This makes a really lovely classroom display and also encourages the idea that one word can represent many different hues.

## Sensory

Adding colour to sensory lessons makes them much more visually motivating and interesting to explore. You can, for example, add food colouring to spaghetti, pasta shapes, shaving foam, hair gel and dry rice.

I play a DVD called 'A Sense of Calm' in the background of our sensory sessions. It creates a relaxing atmosphere and relaxes the children as they explore the sensory. Playing the same DVD also sets the scene and structures the session. When the segment is finished we start cleaning up.

## Case study

Rhianna had emerging speech. She would sometimes sing familiar theme tunes, such as 'Bob the Builder, Can You Fix It?', but never engaged in conversational speech. She would opt out of lessons in a quiet but definite way and often get 'stuck' *en route* to different places. She spent the majority of her time in the corner of the classroom, in the corner of the playground or in a corridor.

The observation: One thing that came out of watching Rhianna was how expert she was at opting out and how incredibly definite she was about it. Two things that did get a spark of interest were the interactive whiteboard and watching cereal being poured at snack time. She didn't want to touch it or eat it, but she was entranced by watching it pour. When the box was left unattended, Rhianna was there with lightning speed, pouring the contents all over the table.

The investigation: After a long chat with Rhianna's mum, I found out that she liked watching things pour at home too. Everything had to be locked away high out of her reach to avoid it being poured. Rhianna's poor mum – I could only imagine…

Getting creative: We made a selection of sensory trays for Rhianna to explore – pasta, sand, glitter, rice and flour. Rice was the clear winner. The rice tray became a great starting point for intensive interaction. Rhianna would even ask for it using her PECs. But rice was the only thing Rhianna would ask for. She had mastered the sentence 'I want rice', but I wanted to see if she could extend her communication.

If only the rice could be different colours perhaps we could get her to use symbols to request a specific colour. We dyed all the rice in rainbow colours and put it in the trays to dry out. Our experiment paid off – Rhianna clearly liked her new coloured rice. She didn't do what I'd hoped, which was to select a favourite colour and ask for it, but she did like watching us add one colour at a time. In time this motivated Rhianna to extend her PECs sentence to 'I want red/yellow/blue/green/orange/purple rice.'

It is vital that we help each child find a subject he enjoys and can develop. Many people with autism have natural gifts and flair for art. They often have a unique way of seeing things and they express this through their art. The autistic artist Judy Endow says, 'If my way of thinking in the movement and sound of color had been supported as a youngster I likely would have been able to produce paintings long before my late 50s. There are so many examples of people with autism making an eventual living from their art. It's an area where they can excel if given the right level of freedom and encouragement' (Endow 2012).

And let's not forget that art can also be a good way to wind down and relax. The art does not have to be gallery worthy. The feeling the person gets from doing the art can be more valuable than the art itself.

# Chapter 10

# Defining Space through Colour

'To be yourself in a world that is constantly trying to make you something else is the greatest accomplishment.'

Ralph Waldo Emerson

You are in a bubble. It contains fresh, unpolluted air and a specially adapted environment. Not everyone can see your bubble. The fine wall is only visible if it catches the light in a certain way… Oh, and the slightest little touch will cause it to pop. You can only guess what the consequences would be.

We all have our bubble. There's an invisible line that we don't like people to pass. If someone gets too close, we will naturally take a step back. In addition, our bubbles have layers like an onion. We expect people to know which layer applies to them, but this can be complex. We anticipate that a stranger will know to stand further back than a close friend. Our best friend can walk in and give us a huge hug without bursting our bubble, but if someone we don't know did this, our reaction would be different. Personal space might be instinctive to us, but many children (particularly those with ASC) do not have the innate ability to define those space boundaries. So it's up to us to help them learn.

There are many ways to teach children about personal space. We could go out in the playground and draw a chalk bubble around each of them or give them each a plastic hoop. We could use pictures of different situations, with a coloured circle representing personal space. The earlier we address the issue of personal space, the better because we cannot assume that this is a natural instinct which will kick in over time.

You may find the following ten tips are useful for teaching about personal space:

1.  Use spots on the floor to teach children how to line up or find a space.

2.  Use carpet squares so that each child has a physical personal area on the floor.

3.  Use coloured tape or hoops to define personal space visually.

4.  Refer to visual symbols for good lining up, walking or sitting.

5.  Role-play and use Social Stories™ to explain instructions such as 'Find a space.'

6.  Structure times between activities so the child has something to do.

7.  Model what to do and use support staff to help.

8.  Display photographs that model correct spacing.

9.  Use visual rewards and praise when children get it right.

10. Wait until *all* the children are in their space before moving on.

## Case study

Ronnie loved being first. It was the most important thing. He would rush through activities and wolf down his snack. The focus was all about being first. I was concerned that Ronnie or another child might get hurt in the rush to always be at the front of the line at the door. We needed to create some structure fast. We began by defining space for lining up by using floor spots. A chart on the wall showed the children which colour spots to stand on. I had laminated the children's photos so we could swap them each day. On the first day I put Ronnie first on purpose. Of course he thoroughly approved of our new system! Children further back in the line were rewarded with praise, tokens and stickers. We waited until all children were in line ready to go. This meant our class was not first out to play that day. Ronnie noticed this, but he was used to us not being first class out.

Next day, I moved the photos so Ronnie was third in line. He clocked this the moment he walked in through the door. 'I'm red today?' he asked to be sure we had not changed the photos by mistake. 'It will change every day Ronnie. That is fair,' I explained. Ronnie amazed us all and totally accepted our new system. I didn't even need the Social Story™ I'd prepared! Sometimes all a child needs is some consistent visual structure.

Using a visual floor spot marks a personal space for the children and helps them learn to stand slightly apart. Furthermore, colour can help them to follow the correct order if you want to ensure that the fastest child is not always the first in line. Allocate a colour to each child or prepare a wall chart showing the children which colour spots to stand on today, as in the case study above. Mix up this order each day. If you prepare the chart before the lesson, when the children are not in the classroom, even better – the children will enjoy discovering where they are supposed to be. There will be fewer arguments if the chart tells them what to do. Make it fun!

My advice is to start off using coloured circles for floor spots. If not all the children are able to make the link with a chart, you could have a duplicate set of circles and give one to every child before the class lines up to show them where to stand.

*Figure 10.1 Shape floor spots*

The shape floor spots shown in Figure 10.1 can be used in numeracy lessons. What a great plenary in a lesson on shape if you are telling a child to stand on a three-sided shape, or a shape with four corners or just a blue shape. This provides so much opportunity for assessment! Floor spots do not have to be arranged in a line. They can be arranged in such a way (e.g. in a circle) so that there is no 'first' and 'last' as shown in Figure 10.2.

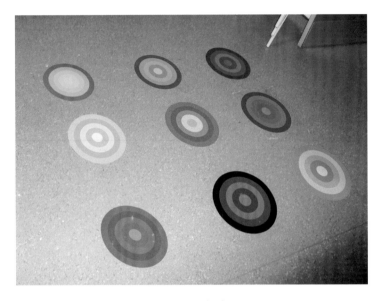

*Figure 10.2 Circle floor spots*

Colour can help order larger groups as well. Floor spots in the playground show the children where to stand when the bell goes. Each class has a different colour set of spots. The classes can then go indoors, one at a time. This saves having a big crush of children at the door when the bell goes.

Spots can be used in a variety of tricky situations, including:

- transitions

- playtime

- carpet time

- lining up

- choice time

- in the car

- on the sofa

- on the trampoline

- party games

- waiting in queues.

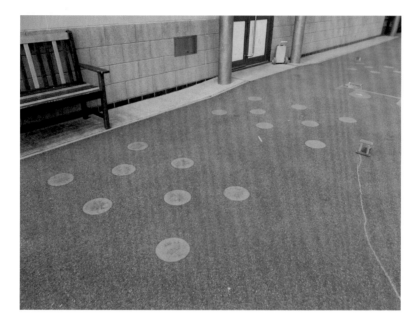

*Figure 10.3 Playground floor spots show children where to stand when the bell goes, avoiding a pile-up at the door*

Remember that not all children are born with awareness of personal space. Up until they start nursery this may not have been an issue. Being at home with Mum is different to having to negotiate a group. Mum may have been a personal climbing frame, a swing bar or a seat and the child needs to learn that climbing on other adults or even children is not acceptable.

There will be moments when it seems frustrating that a particular child can't seem to line up, sit still or stay in one place. Children are naturally wriggly and some will only learn about personal space with the right structure and support. If we make learning about personal space visual and motivating, children have a greater chance of success.

## Where do I go?

Often in lessons we split the group. Some children will work at one table, some at another. Coloured tables immediately give them a visual as to where you want them to be, as explained and illustrated in Chapter 3.

A transition board can help a child learn to refer to their timetable and transition to the appropriate area. The child goes to his individual timetable and takes the symbol from the top or from the left, then matches this symbol on a transition board in the correct location (e.g. on the yellow table). This means that the child has travelled successfully to the next activity. It is important to structure some favoured activities into the timetable to help keep a child on track.

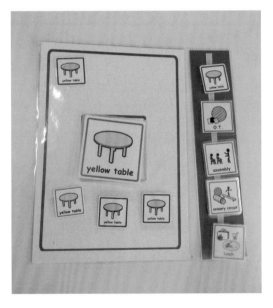

*Figure 10.4 The child takes the yellow table symbol and transitions to the table to place it on the transition board*

An individual schedule will usually be kept in the same place so that a child knows where to go to check it. Schedules can be personalised with individual motivators.

## Choice time

Colour can be particularly helpful if you are trying to structure choice time. Most typically developing children can cope with the idea of choosing. They will naturally do one activity, complete or tire of it and move on.

This is rarely the case for children with autism. They might only really like one thing (e.g. the sandpit). Why would they move on? Colour coding choices and giving children a visual chart shows them they *must* move on and try all activities before returning to the sandpit.

Each time children select an activity, they remove it and post it. Only when they have tried everything will they be able to return to their favourite activity. It's surprising how they accept this and appreciate the structure. Choice time is not actually choice time because the teacher has an unspoken expectation that the children will choose more than one activity. To clarify this we must add structure.

## Where do I sit?

Colour can be a good visual and help sort the children so they don't sit next to the one child who is easy to wind up or who joins in with distracting the group. Just stick a bit of coloured paper to the backs of the chairs or use coloured tape on the chair legs – it's simple, cheap and effective!

We can adapt this to sitting on the floor, using coloured carpet squares. Like the floor spots, these help teach children about personal space. If using floor spots already, another way of arranging seating is to add pictures to the children's chairs that link with the floor spots, so you can pre-arrange where they sit.

Often children with autism gravitate towards the teacher's chair. This is partly to do with testing, but may also be because the teacher's chair is seen as the best one. If you were in a room with a hard plastic chair and a comfy padded one on wheels which would you go for? I'd recommend not having a different teacher's chair unless you need one for health reasons. This removes the issue.

*Figure 10.5 Carpet floor spots can help define space at carpet time*

*Figure 10.6 Coloured benches show the children where to sit in assembly*
The position of the blue benches indicates that blue class will lead the assembly.

## Where am I?

A purpose-built school for young people with autism will aim to be free of distractions and visual clutter, but where every corridor, door and carpet is the same, there have to be some visual landmarks to help the children learn to find their way around independently.

If we link the colour of the classroom doors to the colour of the class spots in the playground, we make another connection. Those children on the green spots are in the room with the green door. To get to the red door they walk past yellow and orange first.

*Figure 10.7 Colour-coded doors can promote independence as they help children navigate their way around school*

*Figure 10.8 A central corridor, known as 'The Street', at New Struan School in Scotland*

New Struan School is purpose-built for young people with autism. 'The Street' is central to the building's design. It runs the length of the building, but is a wide space flooded with natural light. Each classroom has a curved learning space or 'bay' outside, where the carpet colour is used to provide a visual link that may help students transition from 'The Street' into the classroom (i.e. the colour of carpet in the bays continues into the classroom). Colour schemes were researched and planned to promote a sense of calm and to create a positive mood. Dr Peter Vermeulen (Centre for Concrete Communication, Belgium) visited the school and commented, 'New Struan is an excellent example of an autism friendly school and should be considered as an outstanding model of how schools for pupils with autism should be designed. It is a brilliant source of inspiration for other schools.'

Long, wide corridors are often a feature in modern school buildings. As we walk down a wide corridor, we instinctively know to move out of the way or continue on our path as someone approaches. We 'read' the person coming towards us and make a decision. If you watch people with autism, you will see that quite often they are not clear about whether to move out of the way or carry on. Perhaps we should show the direction of human traffic in our corridors in the same way we do on roads. Furthermore, visual signposts for 'good walking' along the way can help reduce the speed of traffic.

## Homework

Older students can learn to better organise their work by allocating a colour for each subject. Let them choose colours by association and then keep papers for that subject in coloured folders. They can also use the associated colour to mark on the planner when homework is due in. If they use sticky Post-it® notes on their papers, they can immediately see which folder these belong in. These Post-its® can also be used as book markers.

A good way of learning to organise thoughts for an essay is to highlight points of interest in a colour as a visual reminder of where that point should go. You can highlight what will go in the introduction, middle and end. You could also use little coloured Post-its® – one by the note and one to mark the page.

## Taking notes and revision

Some students colour code their notes. They work out their own individual system. It means that when they come to revise or read over their notes, they can pick out the most relevant details.

Different coloured files, paper and notepads can help a student link books to each subject. You can add a sticker spot to the spine of associated books. By highlighting or underlining lessons on the timetable, a student can quickly see which lessons they have that day and ensure they have the right books.

## Where do I put it?

Colour-coded boxes for home books, snacks and homework can be seen from a distance, so as the children walk into the classroom they are already thinking about putting the right thing in the right box. By creating this clear visual structure, the teacher helps the children to start taking responsibility and to sort their things independently. The colours set the children up to succeed and the distance allows them time to process the expectation.

### The 'finished' tray

We don't even need to label the finished work tray. Just make it red and the children will soon make the connection. This can also be used at home for homework. When a piece of work is finished it goes in the red 'finished' box.

*Figure 10.9 The position and red colour define the*
*'finished' tray before visual labels are added*

## My things

Some teachers allocate a colour to each child to promote independence. This can also be useful at home. Parents can colour code drawers for clothes so all the children in the family have their own colours. Add a label with an image of what is inside. A lot of children enjoy seeing the structure behind what we do. Even if they are not ready to fold their clothes and put them in the drawer, they like seeing the order and learning where things go. In time, because they understand the structure, they may decide to take control and put their own clothes away.

Allocating a colour to children's belongings can also help them to learn to define what is theirs before they recognise their name labels. Add a small coloured spot sticker to things such as pencils and add a dot in that same colour to name labels.

Visual structures make our expectations clear to children with autism. Things that might seem obvious to us can be confusing to them. These structures will help children achieve independence.

# Chapter 11

# Colour-Coded Planning and Classroom Management

'Nothing strengthens authority so much as silence.'

Leonardo Da Vinci

I allocate each staff member a colour so they can quickly see when they have a specific role at a certain time in the day. I type out a daily planning sheet, then colour copy and enlarge it for the classroom wall. This may sound time consuming, but it actually saves time and makes the day run so much more smoothly. It also makes the classroom quieter and the children are able to focus better without the distraction of adults discussing what they should be doing.

A typed daily plan also gives more detail for children who can read. If you find children are reading your daily plan you can assign them a colour code and add in jobs for them. They will enjoy the responsibility and it will encourage them in their reading. It will also show them that you know their capabilities.

Sometimes we do not know who will be covering staff absence. You can still colour code the substitute and when the person arrives, show her the board and explain that she is represented by a coloured question mark. The system is clear. Similarly, if someone is suddenly off sick we can reallocate jobs within the team if there is no cover.

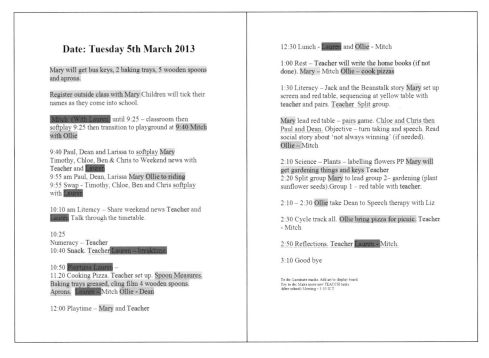

**Date: Tuesday 5th March 2013**

Mary will get bus keys, 2 baking trays, 5 wooden spoons and aprons.

Register outside class with Mary Children will tick their names as they come into school.

Mitch (With Lauren) until 9:25 – classroom then softplay 9:25 then transition to playground at 9:40 Mitch with Ollie

9:40 Paul, Dean and Larissa to softplay Mary Timothy, Chloe, Ben & Chris to Weekend news with Teacher and Lauren
9:55 am Paul, Dean, Larissa Mary Ollie to riding
9:55 Swap - Timothy, Chloe, Ben and Chris softplay with Lauren

10:10 am Literacy – Share weekend news Teacher and Lauren Talk through the timetable.

10:25
Numeracy – Teacher
10:40 Snack. Teacher Lauren – breaktime.

10:50 Playtime Lauren –
11.20 Cooking Pizza. Teacher set up. Spoon Measures. Baking trays greased, cling film 4 wooden spoons. Aprons. Lauren – Mitch Ollie - Dean

12:00 Playtime – Mary and Teacher

12:30 Lunch - Lauren and Ollie - Mitch

1:00 Rest – Teacher will write the home books (if not done). Mary – Mitch Ollie – cook pizzas

1:30 Literacy – Jack and the Beanstalk story Mary set up screen and red table, sequencing at yellow table with teacher and pairs. Teacher Split group.

Mary lead red table – pairs game. Chloe and Chris then Paul and Dean. Objective – turn taking and speech. Read social story about 'not always winning' (if needed). Ollie – Mitch

2:10 Science – Plants – labelling flowers PP Mary will get gardening things and keys Teacher
2:20 Split group Mary to lead group 2– gardening (plant sunflower seeds).Group 1 – red table with teacher.

2:10 – 2:30 Ollie take Dean to Speech therapy with Liz

2:30 Cycle track all. Ollie bring pizza for picnic. Teacher - Mitch

2:50 Reflections. Teacher Lauren - Mitch.

3:10 Good bye

To do: Laminate masks. Add art to display board.
Try to do: Make more new TEACCH tasks
After school: Meeting – 3.30 ICT

*Figure 11.1 A colour-coded daily planning sheet*

## Managing a team

Having high staff-to-children ratios is ideal, but staff must be managed correctly to be effective. You might have four staff to eight children. It's up to the teacher to ensure *everyone* in the class has a motivating day. Keeping staff happy is so important as it creates a happy atmosphere within the class.

By allocating roles in planning you can think of each staff member and quickly see from your colour codes if each one's day is varied enough. You can make sure all members work with a range of students, that they have breaks and that they have a mixture of time indoors and outdoors. Take care of your staff team. If they are motivated and support your methods, your intuitive students will pick up on this. A strong team of adults working together without the need for lots of discussion will make the children feel more secure.

Managing a team is one of the trickiest things we teachers have to do. It can be particularly challenging for new teachers who are still on a learning curve yet have to manage much more experienced and often older support staff. Is there any training for this? There wasn't when I trained…

If you are walking into your first job in a special needs school, be aware. The support staff can be just the opposite of supportive if they do not respect your methods. You must get them on side because they can turn *fast*. They are often highly trained by the school, have a wealth of experience and will care deeply about the children. They will not tolerate being 'led' in the wrong direction if it is wrong for the children. If you do not have a wealth of special needs teaching experience, try to be a little humble and seek the support of other staff and use your teacher mentor. If introducing new ideas or strategies, explain that they are to trial over a set time period.

These colour-coded daily plans, when used over time allow a teacher to perfect the running of the day and direct staff without having to keep asking them. Somehow they remove the issue of being 'told' what to do and show that the staff work as a team. They also highlight that everyone takes turns (e.g. swapping one-to-one staff working with a child in need of additional support). Your expectations are clear and if something is not done, it is obvious to the whole team.

A clearly written, colour-coded plan shows that you have planned the day. Staff can have a look and they can ask any questions about the schedule *before* the children arrive. As time goes on you will not only perfect the running of the day, but be able to dig out last week's documents and amend them quite quickly I also add little notes to the plan if things don't work to remind me next time. My classroom assistant also adds notes for me if there is something I need to remember the following week or if something needs tweaking. Everyone makes mistakes, but if we learn from them that's okay.

On Tuesdays we have what my class call 'swippy swappy' day. We split the group and rotate between soft play and numeracy. In the first week of term I felt dreadful when another group arrived at soft play and my class had not yet swapped. I scribbled a quick note of the swap times on the daily planner and the next week it worked perfectly. How I wish I'd discovered this system in those early days as a teacher. The time and tensions that could have been saved!

As a part of our social context we give individual tutorials to students. A one-to-one tutorial revealed to me how tuned in to colours our young people with autism are. I asked if there was anything different about the way I and the teacher who job shares with me do things (we try to be as consistent as possible). I was informed that I type my schedule but the teacher who job shares with me handwrites it; also that I use colours for people.

I then found out that the student had worked out that I used different colours for the support staff. The funny thing was that when I told the support staff about this tutorial one of them was not aware of the colours (she had joined our team late in the term). I'm certain I always learn more from those tutorials than the students! If you adopt my colour-coded planning for your own class, do remember to tell the support staff. Check you have not used a 'yuck' colour for any of them. Imagine if you hated yellow and you had to spend the whole year looking at your jobs highlighted in yellow. Colours can also have an impact on how the staff feel.

## Job shares

Job shares tend to make staff and parents nervous but they are necessary because teachers will, as they progress in their careers, need to take time away from class. This may be due to promotion (they split being an in-class teacher with being on the senior management team), they take another role within a school or they choose to teach part time to fit in with family.

Job shares work best if you and the other teacher have a similar manner with the children and a consistent teaching style. Excellent communication is essential for a job share to work. If teachers are not afraid to ask each other for ideas, the children can benefit from extra input. When I job share I usually end the day by sending a 'handover essay' email.

## Marking work

The following are some abbreviations to use on pupils' work to show whether or not help was required:

- V/P is a verbal prompt.

- P/P is a physical prompt.

- HOH is hand-over-hand help.

- I is independent work.

When I am marking work with ticks, I use a red pen if the work was independent and a blue pen if the child needed help. The child just sees ticks, but as I return to their work for report writing I see whether or not they could do the work without any help. Without writing anything that would risk lowering a child's self-esteem, the colour tells me if he could do the task with ease or if it's something to revisit and assess at a later date.

Gauge whether to explain your system. The child may be motivated to work independently if you explain.

Add smiley faces to children's work. Looking through lots of work at the end of the year they are really rewarding to see. You may have written a lovely comment, but it could easily be missed amidst a pile of work. Smiley faces stand out.

Encourage children to show their feelings about the work that was set. They can add their own expression faces and a little comment such as 'I found this hard' or 'This was fun'.

## Recording achievements using Post-it® notes

Encourage staff to write 'wow' or special achievements on Post-it® notes. Achievements can be social, physical, personal, communication or academic. A quick note can be stuck to the wall or put in the 'finished' tray and filed later. All this information is great for mapping progress and fantastic to draw on when writing reports.

Post-it® notes now come in all sorts of wonderful colours, shapes and sizes, so if you want a quick visual it's worth making use of these. If the achievement is communication, for example, it could be written on a mouth-shaped Post-it®. Sporting progress could be noted on green, and behaviour on orange, linking with the colours of the symbols. This way, children have another positive visual telling them what they have done to make staff happy. Encourage staff to write these notes in front of the child and add a smiley face. I've noticed that support staff tend to use the shaped Post-it® notes more frequently. Maybe it's not only the children who are motivated by colours and shapes.

## Filing

School filing systems are usually colour coded with set colours for a students' personal notes and academic achievements. The colour coding makes it quicker for a teacher to grab the right information fast when it is needed. A good filing system is essential and a good classroom assistant will help the teacher stay on top of filing by regularly emptying the contents of the 'finished work' tray into the correct files.

## Organising work

Colour-coded trays can help ensure that workstation tasks are changed regularly. You might assign one colour to numeracy and another to literacy. Add the child's name or photo and the trays can easily be changed at the start of the session. Adding this clear visual structure means that you can delegate the job of changing over the trays, safe in the knowledge that the children are getting tasks tailored to their individual ability and interest.

If you are lucky enough to get on a practical TEACCH course, you will see that using a child's individual motivators in individual tasks can encourage independence. In a busy classroom the use of motivators can become diluted and children end up with tasks that are not individually tailored to their interests. The reality is that there is never enough time in the day to make everything perfect. But the more individually motivating the activities are, the better the students perform. Workstation tasks should not be an opportunity to zone out, but a time to be engaged.

## Inspections

Schools in England are monitored by the Office for Standards in Education, Children's Services and Skills (OFSTED). The inspectors call at lunchtime and arrive the next day. They do this so that there is not time to change what is already happening in a school. They may even time the inspection for the day after parents' evening allowing even less time. If you are confident in your school, your methods and your planning, you have little to be concerned about. Yet when a school hears OFSTED are coming, it's like waiting for an imminent invasion. What if they just don't 'get' what you are doing in class?

One of my classroom assistants commented that the colour-coded planning we have on the wall is the sort of thing a teacher might produce when they know the OFSTED inspectors are coming. Don't wait until an inspection is looming – staff need time to adjust and a pupil will most likely give you away during your inspected lesson by asking 'Why have you typed a schedule for today?'

Keep your daily plans in your planning file in case of inspection so that the inspectors can get a clear picture of how you manage each day.

## Observations

All teachers must be observed and monitored for their own professional development. We learn from these observations and have an opportunity to get new ideas. Observations are also an opportunity to zoom in on a particular lesson and reflect on how we teach.

Observations do not feel nice. I'm utterly confident in how I teach the children but when I know I have an observation coming up, I can't help feeling nervous. A good teacher *will* be nervous because they care so much about getting things right.

There's always the possibility that the lesson could go horribly wrong. Children are not predictable and one thing has the potential to shatter a lesson. It does not have to be major. An example springs to mind of when I wrote a child's name beside her work and she had an almighty meltdown because I had written it wrong. I'd written 'Lucy' instead of 'Lucinda' because we all abbreviated her name when speaking to her. As we dealt with the meltdown, I imagined how mortified I would feel if that had been an observed lesson. But these things happen – it's how we handle things when they go 'off plan' that matters. No one will expect all the students to turn into mini saints. If they do, your staffing levels will be questioned.

### Feedback

Even if you do a perfect lesson, you must be prepared for a non-perfect mark. The person observing will be nit-picking – looking for that one thing you could improve on – and sometimes you will be questioned. I was recently observed teaching a colour-coded cooking lesson. It was not hard to prepare as we were just doing what we always do. However, I changed one thing. I gave a student a small bowl of oil to add to their bread. Usually, I would give the tablespoon of oil in the recipe, but I knew the missed learning opportunity to measure would be flagged up. The student added *all* the oil to the bread and this was flagged up with the suggestion of giving only the required amount of oil. Either way it would have been flagged up!

# Chapter 12

# Traffic Lights

'Saying nothing...sometimes says the most.'

Emily Dickinson

I once worked with a little boy with a traffic light obsession. He would do anything he could to manipulate you into using traffic light colours. His perfect day would be spent watching traffic lights. At night he would go to sleep cuddling a toy traffic light.

Here are ten reasons why traffic lights might appeal to a person with autism.

1.  In a puzzling world they are definite (what they say goes).

2.  They control people, cars and even buses.

3.  They can be controlled by buttons – the power!

4.  They have lights – appealing to the sensory.

5.  We can still see them at night. They do not sleep.

6.  They use colours to tell people what to do.

7.  Their rules are understood. They are consistent.

8.  They don't use incomprehensible language or social rules.

9.  If they are red, everyone stops.

10. They make sense.

Traffic lights do indeed make sense. Maybe this little boy had good reason to love them more than a stuffed bear. What had a bear ever done to help him? What role did it have?

When I first began to work with this child, the traffic lights were seen as an unwanted obsession. I could understand that to his parents cuddling a traffic light seemed unusual and they would prefer that he learnt to love something more 'typical'. The boy would try his absolute best to trick us into incorporating traffic lights into his lesson. These colours are everywhere, so it wasn't difficult. What we found was that if we used the traffic light colours, his performance improved dramatically. Suddenly he was interested in sums if they were written in red yellow and green.

We decided to turn the situation to our advantage and use the traffic lights to motivate him. He was happier, behaved better, progressed faster and even seemed less 'obsessed'. This fits so well with what I would later learn from the University of Carolina's TEACCH Autism Program. Rather than fighting the love of traffic lights, we were using it as a motivator to help engage the child to learn.

Benjamin Brittain, who was diagnosed with Asperger's Syndrome, was so fascinated with traffic lights that at the age of 11 he made local news by getting a real traffic light installed in his garden. His mother Jayne explained to BBC News, 'Every time we went out I would look in toy and model shops to see if we could find any but the only thing we found were model signals – and they weren't good enough' (BBC 2003).

Traffic light systems can be effective in teaching people with autism because we are using connections they may have already learnt from taking walks and being in the car. We learn the traffic lights colour code for our own protection. It is quick and efficient. Sometimes we don't have time to read a sign. These colours are instant. They are consistent. They keep people safe.

The traffic light visual (Figure 12.1) can be an effective way to teach children about asking for help. The arrow is attached to a clothes peg and can be moved up and down to indicate quickly to others if help is needed. It is effective with pre-verbal children as it allows them to communicate how they feel. It can also teach the child who constantly seeks approval to work independently as he can pause and self-assess the degree of the need for help.

*Figure 12.1 A child holding a traffic light visual*

As time goes on and the child learns how to use the traffic light and connects the colour, we can make the visual less obvious. The child could have a colour-coded pencil case on display and turn it over showing red if help is needed. (These are already being sold by specialist suppliers because they work well in class.) As time goes on, the child could learn to communicate the need for help by selecting and holding up a red pencil.

*Figure 12.2 A pencil case with different coloured sides*
*can be used to indicate when help is needed*

*Figure 12.3 Holding up a red pencil can be a way for students to indicate that help is needed*

It is important we get these colour strategies in place early so that the foundations are in place. As the child gets older, we can replace them with more subtle visuals. If introducing a new concept to a class, the teacher may want to get a quick view of how well the majority of the children think they get the concept. By giving each child a red, yellow and green card she can ask them to hold up green if they totally understand, amber if they are not sure and red if she needs to explain in another way.

The traffic lights can also be a good visual way for children to find a partner to work with and help each other. Tell the children who to work with. You might want children on red to work with those on yellow, or you may have set up activities for the next stage of the lesson on three tables to give the right amount of stretch to every child. Most children will end up in the right place, but look out for those who try to trick your system or who did not process the original instruction and so held up the first card you asked for. As this will happen, always start by asking for red 'I did not understand' cards first.

Children might want to translate this traffic light system into their workbooks, self-assessing and using a coloured spot to indicate if they want more help.

Some teachers even use a set of traffic light coloured trays for children to hand in work according to how challenging they found it. No child should consistently find the set work too easy or too hard. If this happens we are not differentiating to meet the child's individual needs.

Traffic light visuals are also sometimes used as a quick visual for volume control.

## Reading facial expressions

Tony Attwood suggests that using a traffic light system can help a child with Asperger's Syndrome interpret and respond to social signals:

> When the teacher utters a loud 'Ahem' sound as though clearing his throat, a typical child will know this could be a warning sign similar to the road sign that informs the driver there are traffic lights ahead.
>
> The child needs to look at the teachers' face as though looking at traffic lights – if he or she is smiling, a 'green-light' expression, it means you can carry on with whatever you are doing. If the teacher has a frown, but is staring at someone else, this is an 'amber-light' face, meaning be careful, you may have to stop. If he or she is staring at you with an angry expression, a 'red-light' face, it is the clear signal to stop what you are doing or there will be consequences. The child with Asperger's Syndrome, however, may interpret the 'Ahem' simply as indicating that the teacher has a dry throat and needs a throat lozenge or a drink. (Attwood 2007, p.72)

Attwood suggests that the child should make a traffic light visual with pictures of facial expressions that link to the traffic light colours.

Traffic lights send out such a powerful message – one day as the British football referee Ken Aston was sitting in his car waiting for the lights to change, he had a brainwave…and so the language-neutral caution system of football cards was introduced.

*Figure 12.4 Red and yellow cards are used in sport because colour communicates fast*

This familiar language of colour has been adopted by many teachers to retain discipline in class. Using a red/yellow card system can also prove effective with young people with autism, particularly if sport is of high interest. We must take care that we teach the precise meaning and consequence attached to the cards. We should never make assumptions.

## Traffic lights help build independence transitioning around school

A traffic light system on a tag on a school bag can communicate to school staff if children are able to transition independently or if they may need help. Staff immediately know if a child is capable of 'going' independently to the classroom from their taxi or if the child should 'stop' and wait for someone to accompany him. A yellow spot tells staff that the child is almost independent but not yet consistent (he may need direction).

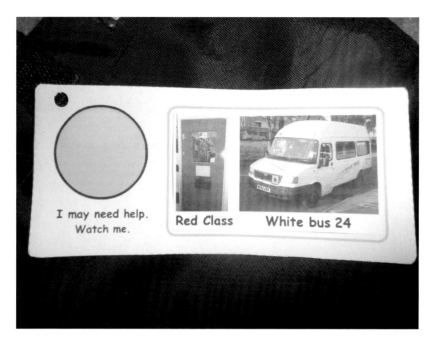

*Figure 12.5 Traffic light tag on a child's bag*

## Lunchtime

Many school canteens now use traffic light systems to help children understand categories and make healthy food choices.

Parents can also use a similar system at home to encourage a healthy variety at mealtimes and in school lunchboxes. Lay out food choices in colour-coded trays or on plates. The child can select any number of healthy snacks from green, a limited choice from yellow, and one from red. A traffic light system helps with order and explanation. It also promotes independence and healthy choices.

A small red circle on a lunchbox can tell lunchtime supervisors that a child will genuinely need help opening it, breaking into packets or tidying things away. A green circle will indicate that a child asking for his crisp packet to be opened should be more independent. Subtle codes like these can provide so much information without the need for verbal explanation. These children do not need to hear adults telling each other what they cannot yet do. The focus must always be on what they *can* do. Less adult chat means less noise, which is another benefit in a busy lunch hall.

## Teacher traffic lights

When teaching a person with autism, create your own traffic light systems. As you get to know the child, you will come to understand how his traffic lights work and how long you might be waiting before you get a response.

Use the following guidelines:

Red: Stop. We present our new idea or question. Stop everything else. If you want an answer, pause what you are in the middle of, sit or crouch so you are at the child's level and use his name before you ask the question.

Amber: Wait. We allow time for the person to process. Waiting might be longer and we might need to add in some extra structure and support.

Green: Go. Maybe we get the expected answer. Maybe we get another answer or perhaps no answer at all. At this stage we go, but we rethink our approach at 'amber'.

Traffic lights are used in so many classrooms in mainstream and special schools. They are a fast visual way to highlight expectations and alert us to problems.

# Chapter 13

# Dealing with 'Different' Days

'There is really no such thing as bad weather,
only different kinds of good weather.'

John Ruskin

Celebrations can be a difficult time for those on the autism spectrum. First, there's the build-up – changes to routine, noise, decorations, waiting, visitors, sensory overload and dealing with emotions like jealousy and disappointment. Then, the celebration day is so totally different and there are a whole load of new rules the child is expected to just know.

## Counting down to special days

No child likes to wait. Autism intensifies the 'not liking' to 'hating with a passion'. When autistic children know that a special day is on the horizon they may need a visual to count down in the same way other children use advent calendars to count down to Christmas. A wall planner displayed somewhere prominent can help them to count down – they do not need to be able to read. You can use pictures or colours to indicate when the special day is. Cross days off as they go so the children can see they are getting closer. Having the special day on the calendar makes it seem more concrete and the children will be less likely to try to negotiate for it to come sooner.

Calendars can become a focus once children realise that there are visual ways to count down days. We know these children like to know what is going to happen next in the day. Calendars can show what's going to happen days, weeks and months ahead. I recall one young boy who had to go around and turn over every calendar in the school at the start of the month. He needed to know that the month had changed throughout the school, not only at home.

Another way to count down is by using a visual. I remember once using fish on the bathroom wall to count down to a special day. Each day, we removed a fish. One morning I heard our son in the bathroom very early. He had woken up and the first thing he wanted to do was go and remove another fish. It was 5am!

## Birthdays

A year seems so long to children. Not only do they have to wait for their own birthday, but in between waiting they have to tolerate other people having birthdays too. All children feel a twinge of jealousy when they see another child getting piles of presents. As with all emotions, autism can intensify the feelings of jealousy into something less controlled. We must have empathy for how intense these feelings are to autistic children. How utterly awful and intolerable it is to see another child being showered with presents but to get none yourself. We have developed a routine that helps a bit. After a party, as one of our sons unwraps his presents, any repeat or unwanted presents are automatically offered to the other child.

I love it when understanding friends give a present to both our boys. There is no set rule that we cannot have a small distracting present for the child who does not have the birthday…as long as we do not make it a routine so that the child expects a present every time someone else has a birthday. Some people might disapprove, but they do not understand how a child's feelings can be intensified.

## Party games

The child with autism may not take losing well. Learning to be a good loser takes time and practice. Try to make it so that losers also win. Make sure the child with autism is not the first to lose so you can show that the child who comes last and loses gracefully gets praise for being such a good sport. Show through the example of other children that it is okay to lose, before the autistic child experiences it personally.

If playing 'pass the parcel', having a little sweet in each layer helps alleviate some of the pain if the child does not win the main prize. Try not to make the main prize anything too amazing. Ideally it will be something the child with autism will not be very interested in. This is not spoiling the child with autism – rather, it is showing understanding of the child and helping him succeed. The other children might have learnt the social rules of turn-taking at pre-school when the child with autism was learning something else.

## Colour-coded presents

Colour coding presents can be a good visual way to let children know what is for them before they are able to read labels. Another great way to highlight who the presents are for is to put photographs of the receivers on the gift tags. Waiting to open presents can be exceptionally difficult for children with autism. If they fail to wait, try not to overreact.

*Figure 13.1 Colour-coded presents show children that not all the gifts are for them*

## Case study

It was a couple of weeks before Christmas and a child in my class had got up early and unwrapped every present and every card. His mum said she had reacted so angrily that she felt guilty, but she didn't know what to do. It was her 'final straw' moment and she admitted she had almost lost it…

Talking it through calmed the situation and helped put things in perspective. I suggested she go for a walk to the shops, buy some new envelopes, then take her list and address book to a coffee shop and re-address the cards. In the meantime I would speak to her son.

Through a comic strip picture I found out that when the boy had unwrapped the presents, it was out of curiosity. He wanted to know what was inside and he couldn't wait to find out. He also wanted to know what was for him.

Why the cards? I don't know. I think that by the time he'd unwrapped the presents it had become a bit of a sensory frenzy and the cards were sat there as another thing to unwrap. I kind of understood.

I spoke to a much calmer mum later on. She said she had gone to the coffee shop. She'd actually enjoyed treating herself to some calm time. She'd posted the cards and put all the presents up in her wardrobe because she wasn't sure what to do next.

We agreed that her son might have a repeat unwrapping session if she was to wrap the presents in the same way. It was too tempting. He had to learn not to open the presents, but we also had to set him up to succeed.

To begin, Mum would wrap the presents again in front of him. She would let him choose one type/colour of paper for his presents. He would then have a visual way of knowing what was for him and the mystery of the other presents would be removed. A few known, non-exciting presents would go under the tree to test if he was able to resist. He would know that none of his presents were under the tree.

After the weekend, Mum let me know he hadn't unwrapped them, so we tested him further. She put a squishy present under the tree (well wrapped, without tempting rippy bits). This boy was very into his Lego®. I knew he wouldn't be able to resist if the present had that telltale sound, but squishy presents are often less exciting. He got lots of praise when the wrapping stayed on.

On Christmas Day the boy's presents were all wrapped in his chosen paper. His mum had also put little photos on the other presents so he could enjoy handing them out. He enjoyed doing this and telling people what was *not* in the package.

I had a well-wrapped squishy present under my own tree that year. I finally got past all the tape and layers of paper and found a lovely sparkly scarf with a very sweet thank you card. I'm not a sparkles person, but I do love that scarf as whenever I see it I think of that lovely mum and I hope she's enjoying a nice cappuccino reflecting on how much progress her little man (who is now in a mainstream secondary school) has made.

## Fireworks

Fireworks – we love them or hate them. People with autism may love fireworks for the colour, the sensory and the excitement. They may also hate the noise, the change in routine and the fact that they cannot see where the fireworks are coming from.

Darkness and light, and day and night happen. We can control the lights in the house, but not the sun, moon and stars. It gets darker and quieter at night. People sleep. The curtains are closed. We bath, we go to bed.

Then there is this one night when it all changes. The sky is full of big bangs and explosions, and huge crowds gather to look at the sky. They should be inside, in bed. This is confusing and can be quite frightening.

Some children find it difficult to stay outside and watch fireworks. Their fear is real. However, we cannot stop fireworks going off at night. They are something so many people enjoy. Fireworks are no longer restricted to once a year. People seem to need little excuse to light up the night sky with a big bang. There are fireworks at weddings, birthdays, New Year, Christmas, office parties.

I spent three years teaching at a school for young people with autism. It has become quite famous (locally) for holding a daytime fireworks display. The reason? There are some pupils who are very scared by the idea and the noise of fireworks. By having daytime fireworks at school they can see the fireworks being lit and anticipate the bang that will follow. We would let them see fireworks in a safe, familiar environment where they are used to facing challenges, new experiences and overcoming hurdles with the support of staff they can trust. It's essential that if a child is frightened by fireworks, we at least show him what is happening in daylight. Remove some of the mystery and we may remove some of the fear.

We encourage, we cajole, and when these children do manage to stay out and observe from a distance, we praise them. Daytime fireworks may seem a little unconventional, but they can be effective in removing some of the fear associated with fireworks at night.

## Colour-coded egg hunts

All children like things to be fair and it's up to us to ensure that a fun activity, like an egg hunt, does not end in a devastating meltdown because some children get more eggs than others.

Give the children different coloured baskets/buckets and let them collect eggs of that same colour. If you think they need an extra colour clue, dress them in corresponding colours or give them colour bracelets. Give children a clear visual cue and you will solve many of the usual issues.

*Figure 13.2 A colour-coded egg hunt*

## 'Non-uniform' days

Every day the children go to school they wear uniform. They have a known schedule, which is usually quite reliable. They know what's expected and what's going to happen.

It may have taken sometime overcoming sensory issues and getting the child to wear a uniform. Then the school decides to throw a spanner in the works by announcing that on 'Children in Need Day' all children should come in wearing pyjamas and bring in £1. The idea is a 'fun' way for the children to raise money. The reality for a child with autism can be confusion, fear and anxiety. I have to admit I don't like these days either. Teaching a class while wearing pyjamas just feels all wrong.

These school dressing-up and theme days seem to be getting more and more frequent. For children with autism they can seem anything but fun. They can also potentially slip a child out of the routine of wearing uniform. If she dressed as a princess one day, why can't she do this every day?

The child wants things to be the same, but even if he sticks to routine and wears uniform he will be the 'odd one out' because the other children and teachers are all dressed up. There's no way of winning! I'm not a fan of these days, but they will happen. They are not only a school thing.

If you have a child with autism in your class, I suggest you send home a little note explaining to the parents that if their child does not wish to dress up, that is okay. They might want to send in the clothes in case the child decides to dress up once in school. You could also use a Social Story™ to explain the day and send a copy of this home.

Build up to the day by showing it on the school calendar. Draw little peg people with uniform written under and then on the 'special' day draw a peg person with the theme clothes. Make sure that the following days show everyone back in school uniform.

*Figure 13.3 A colour-coded calendar indicating non-uniform day*

If children don't want to dress differently, I think we should allow them to choose, but having a visual explanation on the calendar might help them cope with everyone else being different. It will also reassure them that things will be back to normal the next day.

We must do our best to set them up to succeed and always assess if what we are asking of them is fair!

## Dressing for different weather

We need to teach children about wearing different clothes in different weather conditions. They need to know the reasons behind changing clothes. Sometimes autistic children get stuck wearing jumpers and trousers when the weather gets hot because they are in a routine of wearing those clothes and find it really difficult to adapt. We cannot simply expect them to take their jumper off because we ask them to. It will not make sense to them to do so. We need to approach this with Social Stories™, photos and videos that show how people dress for different weather and explain why.

If the parents cannot get their child to come to school wearing shorts on hot days ask them to send shorts in the child's school bag. This way you can have another try once the child arrives at school. Often mornings are cooler, so the idea of shorts may seem illogical early in the day, but make sense later. Seeing classmates in shorts could also make the idea seem less bizarre.

## When the weather changes planned activities

One thing we cannot control is the weather. We must prepare children for the eventuality that the weather can change planned activities. For example, we might have planned a trip to the beach on Friday, but we wake up to rain. We logically decide to cancel the outing to the beach, but this may not seem logical or acceptable to the child with autism. One way to help prepare the child is to use a calendar. Put the calendar somewhere prominent. Opposite the toilet is a good place. Instead of just writing 'beach', split the box on the calendar for that day into two, drawing a sun in one half with the beach option and rain in the other half with a different option. This could be 'DVD' or 'soft play', for example. This will give the children lots of advance warning so that when they wake up to rain, they will already have a picture of what will happen without you telling them. The disappointment will be much easier to handle.

'Wet play' can be another difficult thing to explain, and children may need a visual to understand why they are not going outside. Sometimes it is better to put on waterproofs and take the children outside anyway because they need this outside time in their day.

## Being late

No matter how we try, there will be times when a child is thrown out of his routine by a late night or a late meal. Know the child and make allowances if this affects behaviour. Tiredness and hunger can unsettle anyone. If you know a meal is going to be late, try to add in a snack. If you are aware that a child has had a late night or not slept well, then adapt accordingly by reducing your demands.

## Fire alarms

The fire alarm will go off at some point. Teach the children the fire alarm routine as soon as possible (before the school fire drill happens). Set it up as part of a lesson explaining that you are going to learn about fire drills. Have the fire alarm symbol on the timetable so they know you are going to learn about it. Physically walk through your emergency route. The more the children can prepare, the better, because at some point the alarm *will* go off and it will not be scheduled. It's also useful to have a bag full of individual motivators and visuals prepared for when the alarm goes off for a drill. Take the bag with you when you practise, but only use the contents in actual drills.

The motivators are there for use incase a child has trouble with the unexpected transition or finds the crowds or waiting distressing. They can be used as an incentive to motivate movement or provide comfort or reward. Take the bag with you when you practice, but only use the contents if they are needed. The more they are used the less novel and powerful they may be.

If a child asked what was in the bag I would explain that the bag contained information, and show him the visual symbols and some of the other things that might help his class mates if they found the fire alarm difficult. An enquiring child should be given the truth whenever possible. We must build children's trust and we do this by consistently giving them the truth.

Fire alarms don't just happen at school. They can happen anywhere – the swimming pool, the bowling alley, the shopping centre. We must prepare children with autism for fire alarms in different situations because they will happen. We can do this by having pretend fire alarm drills and pointing out fire exits, smoke alarms and fire extinguishers. Try to make the fire alarm a known possibility so that when it does go off unexpectedly the child has learnt ways to cope.

## Handling a 'whoops!'

Things cannot always go to plan. A school 'whoops!' could be that the swimming pool is out of action, rain prevents football at playtime, the computer crashes, the teacher is off sick, a home book goes missing. These things are inevitable and we need a set of school strategies to prepare the children so they do not have a meltdown. These strategies may include Social Stories™, behaviour management strategies, distractions or alternative activities. If a child does reach boiling point, he needs to know that there is somewhere to go and take time to calm down.

A school postbox can also help since it enables the child to send a message directly to the head teacher explaining what is wrong or simply saying 'I hate school.' Letting this out by writing it down or seeing it written, then physically posting it in a box, will help the child let go of the issue.

*Figure 13.4 A 'whoops!' symbol can show when we accidentally have to go off timetable*

Even if a reaction seems extreme, we must not be cross. Let the child ride out the meltdown, give him space and when instinct tells you it is okay, approach quietly and sit nearby with a written visual showing what is going to happen next. Verbal explanation will not help.

Time calming from a meltdown will sometimes mean the child has missed a timetabled activity and there are children who will not cope well with this. Know who these children are and if they need to do a speedy literacy lesson, read a quick story and go through the motion to tick that box off their list. When we know the child, we can be aware of triggers and ways to support him. In a school setting it is hoped that a child will have a behaviour plan explaining these triggers and suggesting the best strategies. It is vital to read these documents before teaching these children, so that you do not accidentally trigger a meltdown.

Home is even more unpredictable than school. We must set up systems so that when the child faces a 'whoops!', we have some back up. A 'whoops!' could be a neighbour popping in for a chat when we were about to make a cake, a dear friend in mid-crisis calling when we were about to leave for the park, a scratched DVD, a broken toy, having to go to school to pick up a sibling who is sick... There are endless possibilities and these things have a habit of happening at the worst times. The best way to handle a 'whoops!' situation is to try to prepare. Make a list of potential situations and rehearse what you will do. Prepare visuals and teach the child what they mean. An unexpected visitor could mean DVD, computer or tablet time. If you can, stage an unexpected visit with a friend turning up at the door invited, but unexpected by the child. When the friend leaves, you might reward the child if he has coped well, so he remembers the positives next time. Only do this if you are prepared that this reward will be routine for a while.

Try to be prepared – think through situations before they arise. When a 'whoops!' occurs, stay calm and positive so that the child knows you are in control. If you already have ideas, alternatives and rewards, the child will have more reason to stay on track despite the 'whoops!'

# Chapter 14

# Perception

'If the doors of perception were cleansed, everything
would appear to man as it is – infinite.'

William Blake

Imagine you are looking through a window observing a class of children. A little boy comes to your window and puts his face up to the glass right in front of you. You smile at him, hoping for a positive reaction. The boy holds his car up to the window, but he does not seem to see you. The boy is looking in the classroom mirror. He sees the reflection of his car and has no idea you are on the other side smiling at him. There is nothing wrong with his sight, but his perception from the other side of the glass is completely different to yours. The classroom has been fitted with 'Big Brother' two-way mirrors so that the children will not be distracted by people observing them. Once you realise this, you understand his behaviour. You see one way, the boy sees another and the teacher is aware of both perspectives. She knows people may be looking in and may even notice tell-tale shadows moving on the other side of the glass. Similarly, when it comes to meeting the needs of individual learners, the teacher must be aware of the child's perception in order to tailor the approach.

We may set out a host of wonderful toys and exciting activities and feel frustrated when a child chooses to fixate on one thing, but we must try to see things through the child's eyes. Writing about his time in nursery, Daniel Tammet recalls:

> There was a sandpit in which I spent long periods of the day picking and pulling at the sand, fascinated by the individual grains… I remember walking slowly, my head firmly down, watching my feet as I trod around different parts of the floor, experiencing the different sensations under my soles. (Tammet 2007, pp.24–25)

I wonder what Daniel Tammet's teacher made of his behaviour. Did she believe he was one of the bright sparks in the group? If she had to pick out which child in the class would become famous for his 'unimaginable mental powers', would she have chosen him? Should Daniel have been encouraged to socialise more? Should he have been directed to more 'appropriate' toys or shown how to play with diggers in the sand?

What would I do if Daniel was in my class? I would play alongside him, get in there and explore the sand (try to see it though his eyes). I would remove my shoes and explore the textures of the nursery floor. I would add new textures like bubble wrap. Maybe this would spark the interest of another child too and he would see the fun in exploring floor textures. Next, I'd get a big sandpit and walk through it, then bury my feet. I'd genuinely enjoy every minute and in time I'd hope Daniel might notice someone sharing his interests and choose to interact. I'd allow Daniel to lead the investigations. This way we both might learn something.

We are so lucky to have memoirs like those of Daniel Tammet. By explaining how they perceive the world and how they experienced education, adults on the autistic spectrum are turning the tables to become the best teacher teachers, helping us to set up the children of tomorrow to succeed.

Kristine Barnett explains how she would tell parents to try to see the world from their child's perspective:

> If they could get into their children's worlds, instead of expecting their kids to come out, they'd find some beautiful things. It's up to us to build the bridge to our children, so that they can show us what they see and we can begin to draw them back into our world. (Barnett 2013a, p.95)

Searching through chat rooms, memoirs and blogs written by people with autism I found a recurring theme: countless vivid accounts of altered perception, fragmented vision and intense sensitivity to sound, light and touch.

Children with autism often have a fascination with light and shadows. Figure 14.1 shows a child playing with a shadow puppet he created. Making the puppet required him following a set of visual instructions and cutting around lines. He had to complete some rather fiddly steps to get his puppet made, but was really motivated because he had seen what he was working towards. When we look at the puppet we see one set of details. When we focus on the shadow the colours and faces of puppets disappear and the movement of the silhouette become the focus. As I watched my class exploring their shadow puppets I wished that for just a moment I could see through their eyes. We will never be able to see how they see, but having an awareness of differing perceptions helps teachers adopt a more empathic teaching style.

*Figure 14.1 Shadow puppets*

## Sensory overload

One piece of the puzzle that appears again and again is sensory overload. Adults with Asperger's Syndrome report feeling bombarded and overloaded, with distorted vision. They speak of being dazzled by light and colour.

David Mitchell, father of a child with autism, author and co-translator of Naoki Higashida's powerful book, *The Reason I Jump: One Boy's Voice From the Silence of Autism*, explains what sensory overload might feel like:

> Now your mind is a room where twenty radios, all tuned to different stations, are blaring out voices and music. The radios have no off switches or volume controls, the room you're in has no door or window, and relief will only come when you are too exhausted to stay awake…suddenly

sensory input from your environment is flooding in too, unfiltered in quality and overwhelming in quantity. Colours and patterns swim and clamour for your attention.

The fabric conditioner in your sweater smells as strong as air-freshener fired up your nostrils. Your comfy jeans now feel as scratchy as steel wool. Your vestibular and proprioceptive senses are out of kilter, so the floor keeps tilting like a ferry in heavy seas, and you are no longer sure where your hands and feet are in relation to the rest of you. (Higashida 2013, p.2)

## Retreating

Heightened perception can lead to a sense of overload and cause a child to retreat. Temple Grandin explains:

I pulled away when people tried to hug me, because being touched sent an overwhelming tidal wave of stimulation through my body…when noise and sensory over-stimulation became too intense, I was able to shut off my hearing and retreat into my own world. (Grandin 2000)

What if this withdrawal becomes a habit? Rather than arrive at school wondering when they will experience sensory over-stimulation, children cut out that painful step. They arrive and they withdraw.

Carissa Cascio, Assistant Professor of Psychiatry at Vanderbilt University, explains:

If the processing of our vision, hearing, and other sensory systems is abnormal in some way, it will have a cascading effect on other brain functions. You may be able to see better, but at some point the brain really is over-responding. A strong response to high-intensity stimuli in autism could be one reason for withdrawal. (Foss-Feig *et al.* 2013)

Teachers must to be aware of these potential visual distortions and super sensitivities to light, sound and touch.

## Sound sensitivity

Sound sensitivity is one of the first things we might become aware of in children with sensory perception disorder, because their physical reaction (covering their ears) makes the cause of discomfort immediately apparent.

Too much noise can suddenly become overwhelming and cause an otherwise calm child to lose all self-control. We need a way of telling children when they are getting too loud, and using a visual volume control or traffic light system is much more effective than using our voice. The only way of being heard over noise is to be louder, so if an adult raises her voice this adds to the sensitive child's pain.

A child can also use the visual volume control to explain how bad a noise is to him. If the sound of a baby crying is 'off-the-scale awful', we need to know this before we take him to a play park.

*Figure 14.2 A visual volume control allows the teacher or child to communicate about noise levels without speech*

Daniel Tammet writes:

> Ever since I had been able to read I had made my parents take me on a daily trip to the little brick building with graffiti on its walls, and inside, a room with shelf after shelf of colour-coded, plastic-covered children's books and brightly coloured bean bag seats in the corner. The library teamed with quiet and order that always gave me a sense of contentment. (Tammet 2007, p.91)

Autistic people's hearing can be so sensitive that they can tune in to a very distant sound. They might, for example, know by sound alone which car has pulled into the driveway because they have learnt to associate that sound with a particular vehicle. The hum of a fluorescent light could be as distracting as hearing nails screeching down a blackboard.

They might be so tuned in to other sounds that they do not immediately realise when they are being spoken to. Address them first by name so they know you are speaking to them directly. Allow them time to process before they answer.

## Touch
### Clothes

We cannot assume that because something feels a certain way to us that someone else has the same sensory experience. A pair of jeans could feel 'scratchy as steel wool' and, as Naoki Higashida highlights, this can change suddenly because it's to do with perception at that precise moment. One uncomfortable experience with a scratchy label in a T-shirt could make a child believe all T-shirts are scratchy. The child creates a 'scratchy' category when, in fact, another T-shirt could be fine. Making a general rule avoids ever experiencing that feeling again. This can be taken to the extreme with a child not wanting to wear clothes or shoes at all. A child might strip off because clothes get wet in the rain and feel different. Because sensitivity to touch can be such an issue, there are now clothes specially created without scratchy seams and labels.

### Deep pressure

Deep pressure can be extremely soothing to people with autism. Temple Grandin went so far as to create a 'squeeze machine' to get in when she needed the comfort of a squeeze. Children with autism should be able to ask for a 'squeeze' if they need this pressure. One child's comfort squeeze could involve both palms on either side of the head, and to another comfort could come from being wrapped in a weighted blanket like a sausage roll. The child might show you what sort of pressure is soothing by taking your hands and squeezing them or squeezing himself into tight spots. It is so much safer if children learn to ask for a squeeze than go and bang their head against a wall. There are now weighted clothes and even pressure vests available, which can help some of those who have this sensory need.

## Girls with autism

Girls with autism often slip under the net and are not diagnosed in childhood because they are more interested in observing and developing social skills to fit in. Their play may be with dolls rather than sand. They may watch their peers, read fiction, and play out social situations using dolls. Later on, things may unravel and conditions such as anorexia, depression or addiction can lead girls to a psychiatrist who diagnoses autism. Are there really so many more boys with autism or are girls generally more able to get by because their autism manifests in a different way? If you are teaching or parenting a girl with autism then it is worth reading specifically about girls with autism because the condition is often very different with them.

## Brain communication

I began to uncover all sorts of current research into the way the brains of people with autism are wired. Could brain wiring affect their perception?

Investigators from San Diego State University's (SDSU) Brain Developing Imaging Laboratory have identified that in children with autism the connecting pathways were impaired between the thalamus and the cerebral cortex, the brain's outer layer. The thalamus is a deep brain structure that is crucial for functions including vision, hearing, movement control and attention. According to SDSU's Professor of Psychology, Dr Ralph-Axel Müller, 'This impaired connectivity suggests that autism is not simply a disorder of social and communicative abilities, but also affects a broad range of sensory and motor systems' (Nair *et al.* 2013).

Aarti Nair, a student in the SDSU/UCSD Joint Doctoral Program in Clinical Psychology, and Dr Ralph-Axel Müller, an SDSU Professor of Psychology, who was senior investigator of the study, examined more than 50 children, both with autism and without.

> We must take account of altered perception and motor challenges when teaching children with autism. Current criteria for diagnosis focus on the social and communication impairments, but research is beginning to zoom in on the brain and how these children perceive and experience the world. (Nair *et al.* 2013)

169

## Can the brain rewire?

There has been a lot of research about whether people born blind or deaf develop enhanced abilities with the senses that are left.

Though a series of tests on the brains of congenitally deaf cats, researchers found that they were using an area of the brain usually used for processing sounds for enhanced peripheral vision. They discovered that major auditory processing areas in the cats' brains had been rewired to handle visual information. Stephen Lomber, who led the study, stated:

> The brain is very efficient, and doesn't let unused space go to waste… For example, if you're deaf, you would benefit by seeing a car coming far off in your peripheral vision, because you can't hear that car approaching from the side; the same with being able to more accurately detect how fast something is moving. (Lomber, Meredith and Kral 2010)

People born deaf may develop a sort of super vision. 'It seems this area of auditory cortex actually gets reassigned to other senses whether that be vision, or touch' (Lomber *et al.* 2010).

What if the hearing is restored – can the brain return to how it was before? 'The analogy I use', explains Lomber, 'is if you weren't using your cottage and lent it to a friend, that friend gets comfortable, maybe rearranges the furniture and settles in. They may not want to leave just because you've come back' (University of Western Ontario 2010).

While the autistic child is sifting through the sand, could the brain be rewiring itself? He is learning more and more about the science of sand and missing out on the social learning that the other children are engaged in. The peer group is learning how to make friends, share, take turns, dress up, pedal a tricycle, and is developing understanding of social interaction, self-preservation and social context. These are skills that will serve throughout life and children can acquire all of them through play. Their play has a purpose, which is not immediately obvious.

As the autistic brain branches out – analysing, visualising and creating – something has to give. Less brainpower may be devoted to social development. While the autistic child focuses on particles of sunlight that are not even on other children's radar, he misses out on the natural acquisition of social language. Facial expressions, body language and social behaviour, which are all being absorbed by other children, are simply missed in the pursuit of other interests, such as the truth about light and shadows.

Kristine Barnett recalls how her son Jake, because of his autism, 'was afforded much more time in his day than most to focus on the things he cared about: light and shadows, angles and volume, and the way objects move in space' (Barnett 2013a, p.95).

The children playing do not know that they are learning – they are too busy enjoying themselves. This is as it should be. But children with autism want to learn. They do not want to waste their time with noisy social interactions when they could be exploring gravity or capacity. They do not realise that the other children are learning too. They are developing another area of their brain.

Removing the sand is not the answer. This would cause sadness, confrontation and distrust. It would not help anything. By sharing their sand play we help these children develop their understanding of human interaction and social relationships. When they do develop friendships, these are often based on common interests. By sharing sand, we show the children that the social world is not out of bounds to them. We are developing friendship skills on their terms. By sharing their interests we are making ourselves seem interesting. Kristine Barnett saw that her way in was stars and planets. What if she hadn't taken Jake's lead and enjoyed the stars with him?

Researchers from the Kennedy Krieger Institute and Johns Hopkins University School of Medicine examined patterns of movement as children with autism and typically developing children learnt to control a novel tool. The findings suggest that children with autism appear to learn new actions differently from their typically developing peers. Dr Reza Shadmehr, senior study author and Professor of Biomedical Engineering and Neuroscience at Johns Hopkins explains:

> If the way their brain is wired is not allowing them to rely as much as typically developing children on external visual cues to guide behavior, they may have difficulty learning how to interact with other people and interpret the nature of other people's actions. (Science Daily 2009)

Scientists at the University of California, San Diego, have found that a preference for geometric shapes over social images can be an early indicator of autism. The study involved 110 toddlers aged 14–42 months (37 with autism, 22 with developmental delay and 51 typically developing toddlers). The toddlers were shown two videos consecutively.

One video showed moving geometric patterns and the other showed dancing or yoga. Eye-tracking technology revealed that 100 per cent of the toddlers with autism spent over 69 per cent of the time observing the shapes. The researchers concluded that a preference for geometric patterns early in life may be a novel and easily detectable early signature of infants and toddlers at risk for autism.

If a toddler spent more than 69 per cent of his time fixating on geometric patterns, then the positive predictive value for accurately classifying that toddler as having an autism spectrum condition was 100 per cent.

The conclusion was that a preference for geometric patterns early in life may be a novel and easily detectable early signature of infants and toddlers at risk for autism (Pierce *et al.* 2011).

Social messages on brightly coloured shapes are more likely to attract the child's attention. The shape stands out and children eventually learn that by copying the desired behaviour depicted within the shape, they get a positive reaction. The sooner this learning happens, the better, because the longer the children will have to adapt and allow the correct behaviour to become more natural.

The earlier children can develop shared play skills, the better equipped they will be for dealing with school. A child may not see the point in playing with what other children enjoy. If no other children shares the same interests as this child, it is up to us to become his play partner. Children with autism do not want to be isolated. They want to be loved. Changing the way we perceive them will free them to learn. We must respect each child's individuality, intelligence and curiosity and find a way to share what he loves.

When teaching children with autism we must be quick to adapt, follow our instinct and go off plan. The best starting point is to find out what they love and try to see it through their eyes. Embrace their differences and guide them through tricky situations by modelling rather than telling them what to do. We must take account of processing time, their need for perfection and the constraints of fine-motor skills. We must never speak down to a child with autism and must always be extremely positive about what he *can* do. Trying is a huge achievement in itself. Adapting our own perception, following rather than leading, and building bridges are all keys to helping the child with autism learn.

Chapter 15

# Coloured Lightbulbs, Overlays and Lenses

'Dream delivers us to dream, and there is no end to illusion. Life is like a train of moods like a string of beads, and, as we pass through them, they prove to be many-colored lenses which paint the world their own hue...'

Ralph Waldo Emerson

Ashley, a teenager with Asperger's Syndrome, describes how he sees the world:

> The world is a jigsaw puzzle to me, and I can focus on only one piece at a time. None of the pieces are joined together – they are moving; vibrating. I have no faces in my mind, no details, nothing whole. I can see one of your eyes or the other, never both at one time, When I look I can see blurred colours that are whirling and sparking. What I see is only hazy colour; pieces; fragments; nothing whole or detailed. In such a fragmented world, I relate to inanimate objects. Don't try to cure me with therapy while never getting around my piecemeal perception. (Irlen 2010, p.131)

It is estimated that 70 per cent of the information people receive is through what they see. Images are then interpreted by the brain. Sight is the dominant sense (Kranowitz and Silver 1998). What if the experience of distorted vision and seeing a fragmented world is common to children with autism? How can we find out? These children so often have communication difficulties and even those with no language delay would be unlikely to alert us unless they were asked. They would not know that their perception was any different to other people's.

I decided to try to find out how likely it was that any of the children I had taught were challenged by visual distortions. My enquiries led me to a survey conducted in 1994 by the Geneva Centre for Autism in Toronto, Canada, which found that 81 per cent of the study group who were on the autistic spectrum reported distorted perception. According to the Geneva report common problems were:

- difficulties with depth perception

- distorted perception of size, shape, and motion

- distraction

- seeing only small details and not the whole

- visual over-stimulation.

(Walker and Cantello 1994, p.4)

The Geneva Centre conducted their investigation 20 years ago and if those findings reflect how the majority of people with autism see, shouldn't we be screening children after diagnosis? How many children are in classrooms where no one is aware they have distorted vision or altered perception? When children have trouble transitioning, could it be because the floor seems to be a horizontal drop and they believe that if they step forwards, it would be like stepping off a cliff edge? The teacher might reassure them and show them a trusty 'good walking' symbol, but would *you* lower yourself down the side of a cliff face without a harness just because someone showed you 'good climbing'?

Descriptions like the following one have made me think about the children I have taught.

Things suddenly appear and jump towards me like they are going to attack me. I feel scared and I panic. I want to retreat from the chaos because it's just overwhelming. I have to look away and only [look] in short glances. (Irlen 2010, p.137)

I've witnessed that look of panic. I know instinctively that the reason why some children find transitions so difficult that they get 'stuck' in the corridor is not behaviour. Descriptions of distortions sound like a nightmare.

Could this be the experience of many of our visual learners? Are we doing everything we can to find out if children are affected? Is there any way of treating distorted vision? If we changed the lighting, for example, could it help children to see the world in a non-distorted way?

There's that famous quote: 'When you've met one person with autism you have met one person with autism.' We should not assume that when you have met one person with any ability or disability that they represent *all* people, but rather there are approaches that we find work for more than one person with autism. When you've met one person who is blind, you've met one person who is blind. There is no single experience of *any* condition. Being 'blind' is not the same for everyone. One major advance for blind people was the development of braille. Was this thought up by a scientist, an academic or a teacher? Actually, braille was invented by Louis Braille, who was blinded by an accident as a small boy. He knew that the blind could read if they were given the right tools. Frustrations with the limitations of the system he was using to read inspired him to invent something new. Two hundred years later, braille is still in use. Not *every* person who is blind will read using braille. There is never one answer or solution, but the more ideas and options we can offer, the more likely we are to stumble upon something that helps. Braille was invented by someone blind. This made me wonder what adults with ASCs might be discovering.

Not *all* children with autism will have these visual problems, but there are so many reports from adults with autism about distorted, fragmented and sensitive vision that I felt instinctively that the autistic community must be using their own investigation and invention skills. What were they discovering?

Donna Williams, an adult with autism, reported that different coloured lightbulbs influenced her mood and her ability to see accurately. She observed that 'The red had me alert and aware and I started to look for things to do within the room instead of staring hypnotically at the mirror or wallpaper' (Williams 1998, p.140).

Having gone through childhood and education coping with visual distortions, Williams started researching solutions. In the mid-1990s she found that Helen Irlen (a leading expert in the area of perceptual processing disorders) was making some incredible progress, helping students with learning difficulties overcome visual distortions using coloured overlays and spectral filters. Irlen's theory was that the brain may have difficulty processing certain wavelengths of light, even though the eye may be normal. This results in a sufferer perceiving distorted images. Those with Scotopic Sensitivity Syndrome (also known as Meares-Irlen Syndrome and Visual Stress Syndrome) reported that the symptoms of visual stress and distortions such as blurring, moving letters and illusions of shapes and colours on the page reduced when the text was illuminated by their preferential colour. When Williams explained the positive effects of the Spectral Filters she started Irlen on a new and unexpected learning journey. He aimed to help people who had learning difficulties with reading by using coloured screens to stop words and letters jumping about. Since Williams, more adults with ASCs have tried the Irlen Filters and given accounts of how they reduced visual distortions. Irlen explains:

> I wasn't surprised that they no longer saw a distorted world with their Irlen Filters. They reported that their world was no longer overwhelming, bombarding and assaulting. Even physical symptoms and anxiety eliminated. What did come as a surprise, however, was the wide variety of other problems that also improved. Each of these individuals experienced significant improvements not only visually, but in their listening skills, their ability to pull thoughts together, and their ability to communicate. (Irlen 2010, p.131)

Donna Williams explains how the coloured lenses helped her:

> We returned for our new tinted glasses. I put mine on. Ian's face was joined together. His eyes and nose and mouth and chin were all held together with equal impact in a single context. His neck and shoulders and torso and legs were also joined, not bit by bit as my eyes moved along, but as a whole picture. I looked around the room and it didn't seem so crowded, overwhelming, or bombarding. The background noise I had always heard before – machine sounds in distant rooms, the hum of traffic, the mutter of people talking in the background – was not even apparent. I felt I was swimming with the tide and not against it. (Williams 1996)

Often children cannot tell us how they see, but according to Irlen (1998), the following behaviours could be signs of perceptual processing disorders:

- Looking in a series of short glances.

- Looking away from visual targets.

- Squinting or looking down.

- Finger flicking.

- Sideway glances.

- Poor eye contact.

- Rubbing or pushing on eyes.

- Being mesmerised by colours, patterns, or light.

- Behaviour changes in bright lights or sunlight.

- Poor spatial or body awareness.

- Light sensitivity.

- Difficulties with stairs, escalators, or catching balls.

- Poor small or gross motor co-ordination.

This list applies to so many children I have taught. Why was I previously unaware? Why are these children not being screened? Why don't we teachers know about this? I wondered if I was being taken in by the reported success of coloured lenses, but then I found respected adults on the autism spectrum talking about their personal experiences.

Adults with autism would be the first to report truthfully if something did or didn't work. They are by nature seekers of the truth. Many have reported incredible improvements in what they see, once they have discovered coloured lenses. The autistic author and speaker Paul Isaacs documents his first experience after getting his Irlen lenses:

> As I walked around the sitting room things seemed and were more 'connected'. I felt connected in my environment, after years in which I felt so detached and 'foreign'. I looked at objects I found hard to process, such as a small tree in my back garden. I said to James, 'Oh, it has a middle bit' – what I was trying to say was that the connectivity from the leaves, branches and the trunk were all connected. (Isaacs and Billett 2013, p.39)

Highly respected experts on autism, such as Tony Attwood, recognise that Irlen lenses can reduce sensory overload: 'I know of several children and adults (with Asperger's Syndrome) who have reported a considerable reduction in visual sensitivity and sensory overload when wearing Irlen lenses' (Attwood 2007, pp.286–287).

Temple Grandin states on her website:

> Irlen colored lenses help many children and adults. The child or adult tries on many different pale colored lenses until the best color is found. Each person has to find the right color that works for them. For families on a budget, try different pale colored sunglasses at a local store. Often the color that often works best is pale lavender, pale tan, pale pink, and other pale colors… If you are not on a budget, I would recommend going to an Irlen provider who is skilled at helping people find the right color. (Grandin 2012)

*Figure 15.1 Paul Isaacs provided these images to illustrate his perception before and after wearing Irlen Spectral Filters*

Paul Isaacs describes the experience of looking at faces without his tinted lenses:

> I have Prosopagnosia (Face-blindness) with my Autism. I see faces (without my tinted lenses) as a pixelated mass of raw colours that ping into my consciousness, but I cannot begin to comprehend a face nor remember – it's far too complicated. I try and remember people by their voice and if I could touch their face I would remember through my hands as I have no visual memory. (Paul Isaacs, personal communication, 2013)

I do not think any child should go through education coping with these visual distortions if there is a way he might be helped. Adults like Donna Williams and Paul Isaacs are pioneers who have discovered something that helps them and they have documented it to alert parents and professionals. There is an 'Autism Questionnaire', 'Self Tests' and a 'Coloured Lights Activity' on the Irlen website, which could be starting points if you wish to explore this further.

Irlen screeners are certified to administer the first testing session and determine whether an individual will benefit from further evaluation for Irlen Spectral Filters. There are thousands of Irlen screeners worldwide, but if distance or finance prevent access to screening then it may be worthwhile experimenting with different coloured overlays, coloured light bulbs and less expensive tinted glasses.

Research like the Geneva report, and personal accounts of adults on the spectrum, suggests that distorted or fragmented vision could be an issue for learners with autism. A 1996 study carried out at the Institute of Optometry, which called for more research on Meares-Irlen Syndrome, concluded:

> Our data suggests that pattern glare is most likely to be at least part of the mechanism of Meares-Irlen Syndrome. Binocular and accommodative anomalies seem to be often associated with Meares-Irlen Syndrome and it is good clinical practice to treat any clinically significant conventional optometric anomalies as a first priority. Only if the effects remain should the effects of coloured filters be investigated. Our data suggests that these ocular motor anomalies are most likely to be a correlate of Meares-Irlen syndrome, rather than the sole underlying cause. (Evans *et al.* 1996, p.294)

More extensive research is vital to find out how many people are affected and how many could see improvements. In the meantime, teachers should be made aware of visual stress symptoms and the potential difference coloured lights, overlays and lenses could make to a learners perception.

Secondary effects of visual distortion can be poor academic performance and difficulties with everyday functioning. If a child is not able to achieve because of visual distortions this could lead to frustration and fear, which in turn may lead to withdrawal or challenging behaviour. If coloured lenses can potentially stop the world seeming fragmented and put an end to nightmare distortions then the learner with autism who shows signs of visual stress deserves to be screened.

# Chapter 16
# Synaesthesia and Autism

'The world is full of magic things, patiently
waiting for our senses to grow sharper.'

W.B. Yeats

Judy Endow was diagnosed with autism and institutionalised as a teenager because of her behaviour. She is now a self-employed artist, public speaker and mother to three sons. Here she describes how having synaesthesia affects her perception:

> Always, I have a front row seat to watch the show! Each color, with its infinite variety of hues and brightness, has its own movement patterns and sound combinations. Even though spoken words are the medium most often used by people to *communicate* with me, I am wired to connect to these words through the sound and movement of colors. This is the way I think. It moves quite fast, but even so, tends to be slower than the speed of conversation. This can cause me to look less intelligent. People say I have processing delays. Painting allows me to show my thoughts without the burden of constant translation. (Endow 2012)

Is Judy's way of thinking a window to the way other learners with autism may perceive the world? If their perception is faster, brighter and more intense, how might this affect their learning style? Words like Judy's are often echoed in accounts by other adults on the autism spectrum. You might think her description would be unique, yet amidst my ever-expanding pile of autism books it seems more usual than unusual.

Ron Kurtus is the founder of the 'School for Champions' website, and author of 'Tricks for Good Grades'. 'Synaesthesia' is described by him as a 'condition in which the real information of one sense is accompanied by a perception in another sense… A person with synaesthesia may see colours when hearing a sound or may experience a smell when seeing a certain colour' (Kurtus 2004).

I am certainly not the first to connect synaesthesia with autism. Professors at the Autism Research Centre at the University of Cambridge are currently investigating the link. They have already been able to reveal:

> We identified a chromosomal region linked to synaesthesia that has previously been linked to autism, which is the first piece of evidence for a connection between the two conditions. We are now investigating this potential connection and the accompanying implications for our understanding of both conditions. (Asher *et al.* 2012)

If autism and synaesthesia share a chromosomal region and are linked in some way, then perhaps we can use this information to improve educational experience and the chance of future success. We cannot know for sure how many people with autism are also synesthetes, because so many of these individuals will not communicate to a level to be able to explain that they see music, numbers or letters as colours. Research is also being done around the many incidences of known autistic savants having synaesthesia. (However, we don't know how many people with autism have hidden savant abilities.)

Simon Baron-Cohen is the Director of Cambridge University's Autism Research Centre. He is a Professor of Developmental Psychopathology and has written a number of books based on his research. He states:

> Currently it is not known how rare or common it is to have both conditions.
>
> We wish to encourage other clinicians or researchers to document such cases in order for us to understand if they are related in any way. If each condition separately has a prevalence of 1%, and if these were truly independent, then the probability (p) of them co-occurring would be calculated using the multiplication law: p (synaesthesia) x p (autism) = $0.01 \times 0.01 = 1$ in 10,000 (i.e. quite rare). However, if they share some common causal mechanism, such as neural overconnectivity (Baron-Cohen, Harrison *et al.*, 1993; Belmonte *et al.*, 2004), then they may co-occur more often than chance. (Baron-Cohen *et al.* 2007, p.2)

When Daniel Tammet set a European record for reciting Pi in 2004, he captured the attention of Baron-Cohen, who then diagnosed Tammet with Asperger's Syndrome (Tammet 2007, p.7). In fact, Tammet has Asperger's Syndrome, epilepsy and synaesthesia.

Could a significant number of people with autism have brains that are wired in such a way that they are acutely tuned into colours? Jeanne Brohart has written several books, which she has published online. She has shared her extensive research and personal experiences caring for her son Zachary, who has autism. Inspired by her son's relationship with colour, Jeanne Brohart asked on forums about colour and autism. She was contacted by an adult on the spectrum who explained that he had learnt the alphabet by assigning each letter an individual colour (Brohart 2002). Was this adult a synesthete?

I, too, searched the internet, and found many posts by adults on the spectrum describing their personal experiences of synaesthesia. EstherJ posted this reply in a discussion on the 'Wrong Planet' forum. The discussion thread was autism and synaesthesia:

> Synaesthesia does not come with problems on its own…but if you have trouble processing senses, then it can aggravate that issue. For me, I have Sensory Processing Disorder, and my sense of hearing is astronomically sensitive. Thus, I hear EVERYTHING. So, my synaesthesia can aggravate it and make me overstimulated. But it's not the synaesthesia that is the issue. (EstherJ 2013)

I have been wondering at the regularity of such descriptions. How many adults and children with autism cannot explain, but have some form of synaesthesia making them perceive the world in a unique way? People with synaesthesia can reach adulthood without realising there is anything different about their perception. If no one tells them they see or think differently, how will they ever become aware?

Searching for more information I went to the 'Wrong Planet' autism forum. Clayton Brannon explained his synaesthesia to me in a direct message:

> I am only 13, but I have had synaesthesia my whole life. I only found out what synaesthesia was when I was 12, and did further research and concluded I have lexic synaesthesia. I am affected by it as it gives numbers and letters colors (e.g. E is yellow, 4 is green, 5 is lighter green, S is blue, etc.) and each sound also has its own color and geometric pattern. If you play a music file on Windows Media Player, where it shows the fancy

color shows, that is what it looks like in my head pretty much. But, with the letters, it is pretty cool, and with numbers it is amazing, as I am profoundly gifted in math partially because of it. I remember formulas and equations simply by sequences of color. If I really needed to, when I was in public school (currently home/online schooled) I could have drawn kind of a rainbow sequence of colors to remember an equation during a math test on my arms, and the teachers wouldn't have thought I was cheating, as the average student doesn't have synaesthesia. (Clayton Brannon, personal communication, 2013)

How likely, then, is it that I have taught a child with synaesthesia? Are these description of mixed-up senses bound up with colours part of my autistic learners' make-up? Were any of them connecting their colours with letters, sounds or music? If so, was my teaching helping or confusing them?

Synaesthesia can also lead to difficulty processing language and sensory overload.

There is growing evidence that the simultaneous perception of normal synesthetic precepts results in perceptive and cognitive dysfunction affecting linguistic and numerical processing and in severe cases sensory overload can interfere with the ability of affected individuals to lead a normal life. (Asher *et al.* 2009, p.279)

Is it possible that some of our complex pre-verbal students are experiencing sensory overload linked with hidden synaesthesia?

How likely are our visual learners to also be synesthetic? As I continued my research I found so many cases linking synaesthesia and autism. People with autism do not all have synaesthesia, but are autism and synaesthesia likely to co-exist in the same way as autism and epilepsy?

Intrigued, I asked Kristine Barnett if she believed her son Jake had synaesthesia. She replied:

I do think that he has some form of synaesthesia. In fact *Psychology Today* in the US did an article about his synaesthesia even though he has never been diagnosed. I think that although we have not gotten too far into this subject with him…the way Jacob sees the world is like a kaleidoscope of shapes and colors and art that form the equations he so loves. It is a very beautiful way of seeing things! (Barnett 2013b)

Synaesthesia can lead to exceptional skill, such as being able to memorise the phone book, because the person recalls the numbers in picture/pattern form. But as with most gifts, there is a flip side and synaesthesia can also cause confusion. For example, if bus numbers are colour coded, an adult with synaesthesia might get on the yellow number 9 bus instead of the number 7 because the numbers are not coloured to match their 'synaesthesia meme'.

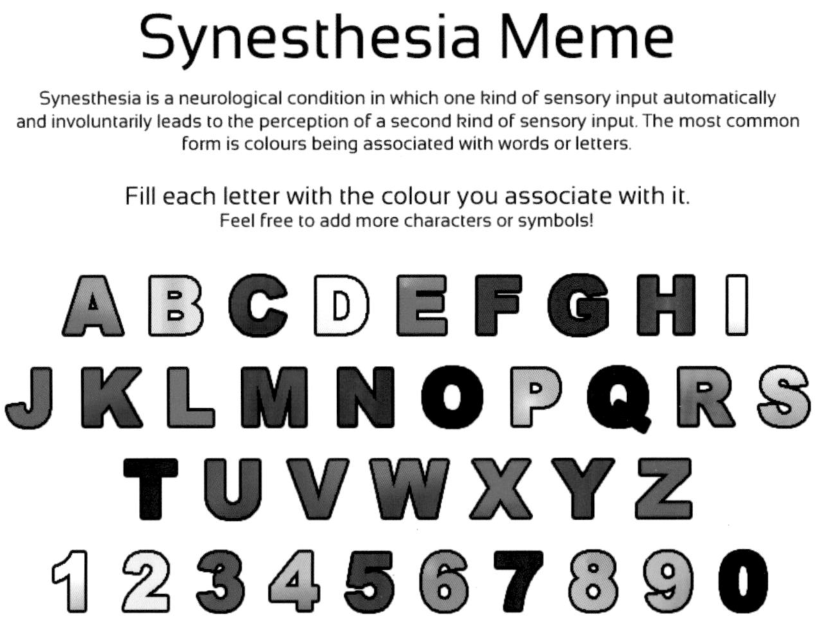

# Synesthesia Meme

Synesthesia is a neurological condition in which one kind of sensory input automatically and involuntarily leads to the perception of a second kind of sensory input. The most common form is colours being associated with words or letters.

**Fill each letter with the colour you associate with it.**
Feel free to add more characters or symbols!

A B C D E F G H I
J K L M N O P Q R S
T U V W X Y Z
1 2 3 4 5 6 7 8 9 0

*Figure 16.1 This synaesthesia meme was coloured by the author*
*Luna Lindsey, who is diagnosed with Asperger's Syndrome*

Luna Lindsey is an author of several e-books who also writes a regular blog explaining her experiences with synaesthesia. She was diagnosed with Asperger's Syndrome in 2013. Luna Lindsey completed this synaesthesia meme and wrote:

I can't tell you how satisfying it is to look at the page and physically see how the letters *should be*. How they are *meant* to be. Not these black pretenders everywhere… I can see into your hearts, all of you, and these are your true colours.

I agonised to get these *just right*. Some of these letters I didn't get just right, and they're glaring at me. (Shut it, 'B', you came early on before

I'd figured out the software, and the tan shades are the hardest to find in the colour tool!)

Note that none of my letters actually have a black border. I would prefer removing them, but that would require more graphics skills than I have. :) Lowercase letters are the same colour as uppercase, though some are slightly different shades.

I shaded some of the letters to help show the motion they have. These are the letters that roam about, swirling or morphing through these particular shades. A few will change a lot. 'I' is the hardest to pin down, since it can be a still, solid white, grey, or bluish-greyish-morphy-whatever.

All of my letters will influence one another when they sit next to each other in words. That's when things get really interesting. (Lindsey 2012)

It may be interesting to give a child with autism a meme. Give him a sheet of paper and have one yourself. Make sure you have a vast choice of colouring pens available. Oil pastels or artists' chalks also work well as they can blend. Begin to colour the letters and see what the child does. Does he just colour his own sheet or does he try to influence you to use certain colours?

If the child shows an interest in selecting colours, repeat this activity some weeks later without looking at the colours used previously. Someone with letter/colour synaesthesia would choose the same colour years later. But that this is just one form of synaesthesia.

What is the likelihood of autism and synaesthesia occurring simultaneously if they are not somehow linked? A 2013 research project, involving 164 people with autism and 97 control subjects who completed questionnaires, revealed that 18.9 per cent of those with autism also had synaesthesia, compared to 7.22 per cent of the control subjects (Baron-Cohen *et al.* 2013). The adults that took part in this study were able to self-assess and complete these questionnaires, but what about people with autism who cannot? Might it be possible that there is greater prevalence of hidden synaesthesia in those with complex autism when we know that it can cause sensory overload, confusion and withdrawal? The report states 'It will also be interesting to test if the current results extend to children with autism, or to more impaired individuals with autism, since our sample only included high-functioning adults' (Baron-Cohen *et al.* 2013).

The most current research concludes that a high percentage of people with autism are also synesthetic. Knowing this must influence our teaching.

Imagine teaching phonics in a class of children where children are hearing different sounds or the letters are coloured wrong according to the child's colour code based on synaesthesia. Children with autism often learn to read visually rather than learning the sounds. Is it possible that some children could associate the word with a colour code and then categorise it so when it is shown again they remember? Given the way adults like Daniel Tammet describe their number knowledge, this seems possible.

I'm not suggesting that all people with autism have synaesthesia, but research shows the conditions often co-exist. We must teach with an awareness of synaesthesia. If a child has synaesthesia, we must help him use it as a stepping stone, but we must also be aware of its potential to become a stumbling block.

# Chapter 17

# Colouring a Brighter Future

'I'm a success today because I had a friend who believed
in me and I didn't have the heart to let him down.'

Abraham Lincoln

Given the diversity of the autism spectrum, it is a startling statistic that only 15 per cent of young people with autism are currently in full-time employment. Schools are trying to address this by focusing on independent work skills and reducing dependence on prompts.

Tasks are structured in a visual way which often includes matching shapes and colours. In time we hope that students will build up to following a set of written instructions, following a schedule of tasks as they might in the workplace.

Our students respond well to all these structures and in time learn to sit at a workstation, completing a set number of familiar non-taxing tasks similar to those shown in Figure 17.1. They are working independently and are not asking for help at each stage, but are the tasks themselves helping to prepare the children for future employment? Are tasks tailored to their skill set and individual interests? It is possible that some students have learnt to use this workstation time as a welcome opportunity to zone out. If we are going to use workstations, the tasks must be kept fresh and also stretch the children so that they still need to think. Tasks must also be based on the students' individual interests.

Teachers who have been on a TEACCH course will have seen the ideal scenario with everything set up for the individual child. If a child's high interest subject is dinosaurs, he will have an activity matching or sorting dinosaurs, with dinosaur pencils and T-rex tokens. This approach is highly effective because the child looks forward to seeing what the next dinosaur activity will be.

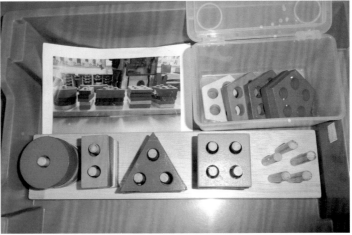

*Figure 17.1 Colour adds structure to these tasks*

## Don't forget the dinosaurs

Despite the best intentions, there can be a problem when it comes to translating this scenario to the classroom. When time and budget constraints are added, the ideal becomes more difficult to achieve and the workstation becomes more functional than motivational. The most depressing workstation task I have seen involved a tray containing plastic nuts and bolts. The expectation was that the child would put them together one day and undo them the next. This may sound soul destroying, but autistic children might simply do this day in and day out because, while they are doing it, the classroom is quiet and they can escape into their own more interesting thoughts. The nuts and bolts task might seem to relate to a future work skill and might be developing fine-motor ability, but what message is it giving children about how we perceive their intelligence? These children are bright – they have so much potential and they deserve to have time invested in their future. The way in is their 'dinosaur'. Don't give them inset puzzles or nuts and bolts because they accept them without making a fuss. As Temple Grandin says, 'You have got to keep autistic children engaged with the world. You cannot let them tune out' (Autism Research Institute 1996).

These children sometimes seem to be trapped behind a series of locked doors, but tapping into their high interest is one of the keys that will help us reach them. The more persistent we are, the closer we get to freeing them to live an independent life and reach their potential.

To put this another way, when a mother is giving birth, each contraction brings her closer to seeing her baby. Each contraction widens the birth canal, eventually allowing the baby to escape the womb. Each time we make a breakthrough, it is like one of those contractions – a small step towards freeing the child. Just like contractions, these steps can be painful. We might have to ride out some almighty tantrums, but when a mother holds her new baby, does she think about the contractions and measure if they were worth it? There is no one answer, no magic pill or therapy, but lots of small steps. We can never ever give up.

## Overcoming barriers and inflexible thinking

Scott James is a young adult with Asperger's Syndrome whose voice talent was discovered on the UK's *The X Factor*. Scott has a fear of travelling by bus because there might be a baby on it. That baby might cry and he finds the crying sound painful. When I asked Scott about whether he would like to get a job, he said that he would like to work but the baby on the bus prevented him from doing so. He said that the ideal situation would be if he could work from home on his computer. In Scott's mind unpredictable babies have become a major obstacle. (Interestingly, before I asked Scott this question he had travelled for half an hour in my car with my baby daughter in the back seat.) This type of barrier can stay with people with autism and prevent them from getting a job. They will not explain their difficulties unless someone asks them, and if we don't know the problem we cannot help them resolve it. Scott's bus issue should have been revealed and tackled through structured support, Social Stories™ and experience while he was still at school. It may not be on the curriculum, but tackling individual anxieties and breaking down barriers is more valuable to an individual with autism than learning algebra.

Scott hated school. In fact he said so many of his behaviour issues at home were the result of anxiety at school. I asked him if there was anything that could have made school better for him. He said that the worst thing was PE – the getting changed and being body conscious and then being less able than other children to do the activities. What if a teacher had asked Scott this question and it had been agreed that during PE Scott could go on the bus to the sports centre and find a sport he enjoyed? They could have tackled the baby-on-the-bus issue and built a positive attitude to sport, which could lead to a healthy lifestyle. Scott and his mother knew that this would not be a possibility. It would have meant communication, expenditure, extra staffing and time, and seeing Scott as deserving a totally individual education. Are these not the very things that should be put in place for a child with a diagnosis? If Scott had been able to access this 'outside-the-box' sports programme, might he now have a regular healthy routine of going to the sports centre and would the baby on the bus still be a barrier to getting a job? Unemployment, obesity, depression and self-medicating through drugs or alcohol are all potential dangers, but they are avoidable if a child has access to a truly individual education.

Judy Endow explains: 'Much trouble occurs because our thoughts are a picture in our heads. When one little thing changes we have to tear down that picture and start from scratch. This is one reason we protest change!' (Endow 2012). For example, a child who always takes the same route when walking to the park might become extremely anxious and protest if asked to take a different route because in changing the route his picture has been 'torn down' and without the picture he is lost.

Endow suggests we use layers of acetate to explain change visually because if a picture is layered, it is not necessary to start from scratch. Using layers of acetate in a folder with visuals, we can show that even though we are taking a different route we are still heading towards the park. Once people are able to create their own visual layers, they can apply this to other situations.

Avoid pictures becoming too concrete by adding in change from the start. Don't always take the same route or stay in the same lane on the motorway or have the same type of bread. By implementing changes before the image is built, we create layers at an early stage, which helps as we add new layers later on. We must not be rigid and bound by routine, but we must explain that we are headed towards the expected destination.

If reactions occur, be empathetic rather than judgemental. Crossing the road at a different place might make sense to you because the traffic lights are broken, but this has ripped down a visual image that could seem catastrophic to the autistic child.

Once we see these things through the autistic child's eyes, we can build supports. A 'good walking' symbol won't help, but Endow's acetate layers would explain so well.

## Colour-coded schoolwork

Post-it® notes, coloured stickers, highlighting pens and coloured filing systems are as essential as pens and paper for taking notes. Once the structure is in place for organising notes and filing, young people with autism will do this naturally but if they start out without any system, they may get to the end of the year with a pile of indistinguishable crumpled notes which are impossible to put in order.

*Figure 17.2 Coloured notes and highlighter pens can help to organise work*

*Figure 17.3 Colour-coded subject files*

Assign one colour per subject and use a sticker in that colour on the spine of related files and books. Do not get the person with autism to do this, but assemble all the files, coloured Post-its® and so on yourself and build the system naturally over time. Introduce the concept as if it's a matter-of-fact choice. For example, 'What colour files are you going to use for science?' rather than 'I think it will help you be organised if you choose a colour for each subject.' (Try to avoid yellow as an option as it does not show up so well in writing.)

When you write down homework or structure a revision timetable, use the relevant colour ink for each subject. This might sound fiddly, but you can make things easy by using a multiple colour biro.

Once young people have learnt to use this system, they can look in their homework diary and quickly go to the right file and match their colour-coded books.

Fionn Hammil is a 13-year-old boy with Asperger's Syndrome, who writes a blog 'autisticandproud' to share how he sees the world with others:

I have a colour-coded timetable with colour-coded folders and books. This makes it easier for me to get my books out.

So this morning at school first period I had English. It went fine.

Then second period was Maths. When I was getting out my maths book – which is Yellow, I noticed my Home Ec book – which is a grey colour. and I realised that I don't have Home Ec today. So I started to wonder what I had forgot.

Then I realised that Home Ec and Geography are kinda similar colours…and I realised I hadn't got my geography folder and book packed.

I went into panic mode. I thought I would get in trouble for forgetting my book – cos it was a TOTALLY NEW EXPERIENCE…in the whole of year 8 I hadn't forgotten my book once.

My options were to show up without a book which I was scared of cos it was a new experience, or I could have phoned home from the office to get it sorted.

I should have told my assistant…and I nearly did…the words were at the tip of my tongue but they wouldn't come out I was so stressed.

I was so scared I didn't think straight.

In our school we are not allowed to have mobiles in school at all, but this was an emergency to me.

So I sneaked to the toilet and I BBMed my dad.

I said I need my geography folder in quick! I felt like on the inside I was about to explode – that was anxiety I think.
I got back into class – still feeling really scared!

But when I looked at my bag again, then I saw my geography folder out of sight and out of reach at the bottom of my bag.

I felt like it was such a relief to just finally see it and for a while I relaxed.

Young people can use a set of coloured Post-it® notes to add markers to the pages of books when they are taking notes for essays. They can use these colours to help with the structure, so the beginning is one colour of Post-its®, the middle is another and conclusions are another. Traffic light colours might be a good choice.

When revising it might be helpful for young people to underline facts they need to remember, using a coloured pencil. As they underline words and formulas, they cement them in their memory and the colour categorises the information so that they can use it for the right exam. (Note: Do not use highlighter over biro as highlighter pens can make the ink disappear over time.)

## Helping adults to organise and prioritise

In the UK, following the All Party Parliamentary Group on Autism (APPGA), it has been decided that educational support should continue up to the age of 25. As effective education often starts later for people with autism and this extra time is essential. I hope this education will focus on overcoming individual barriers so that more young people reach their true potential.

The National Autistic Society website has some really helpful tips, which include the use of colour codes for adults organising and prioritising paperwork, such as household bills.

Colours can be used to indicate the importance or significance of tasks (and therefore help to prioritise tasks and work through them in a logical sequence).

For example, work in a red tray or file could be urgent; work in a green tray or file could be pending; while work in a blue tray or file is not important or has no timescale attached to it (NAS 2013).

There is often an inbuilt facility where you can assign a colour code to emails. This helps with organisational skills and means important emails can be located at a glance. It will also encourage an adult with autism to select emails that are unimportant and can be deleted.

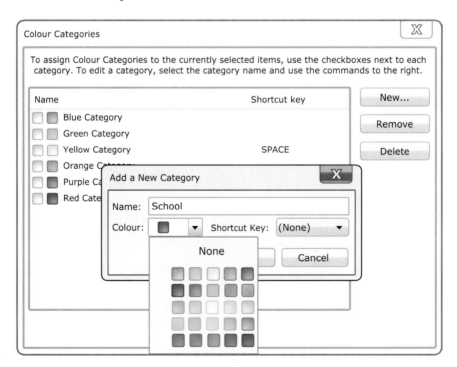

*Figure 17.4 Organising emails by allocating colour to categories*

You can even go into the settings and take this a step further, as illustrated in Figure 17.5.

Using colour associations can eventually translate into the workplace. Colour coding is already being used in working environments for speed and safety. Colour communicates and helps create order. Employees learn the colour code and don't have to take time to read signs. Colour coding is used in many factories where workers speak multiple languages. Rather than translate a sign into 20 different languages, colour is used because colour communicates with everyone.

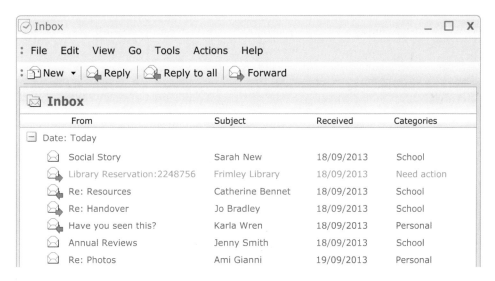

*Figure 17.5 Urgent emails stand out because of colour*

## A positive response to diagnosis

Looking at brain scans can give young people a visual of how their brain might be wired differently. Using this image of Temple Grandin's brain, they may be able to perceive their autism as something positive and beautiful. As you demonstrate how Grandin's brain branches out in certain areas, refer to the young people's individual interests and strengths so it is clear how this brain power is relevant to them.

An internet image search for 'Temple Grandin's brain' could be a effective visual way to show the autistic brain branching out in different directions. Showing this different brain wiring may highlight Grandin's important message: that people with autism may be 'different', but that 'different is not less'.

Diagnosis might feel like a door closing, but with the right support it can open a window, allowing the softest sunlight to pour in.

## Chapter 18

# Final Thoughts and Infinite Possibilities

'To myself I am only a child playing on the beach, while vast oceans of truth lie undiscovered before me.'

Isaac Newton

Some of the ideas in this book might be new, but look around a little and it becomes clear that colour coding echoes everywhere. People respond to colour. It is the simplest, quickest form of communication. Road signs, maps, stamps, uniform and traffic lights all rely on the ease with which people pick up on colour codes. When we need to get information across fast, we use colour.

With access to the right strategies and support, people with autism are more likely to reach their potential. Parents quickly learn that the earlier the child can access intervention, the better, but what is early intervention? What if there is no immediate access to a specialist? I cannot imagine the frustration of being told what your child needs, but not knowing how to access it. The very words 'early intervention' suggest waiting will be detrimental. Parents scour the internet, devour books and constantly seek answers, ideas and strategies that might work. But time spent searching is time taken away from the child. Even if parents save their research for night time, they will probably be exhausted and not in the right frame of mind to read and digest theory. Children's carers are their greatest asset. Parents need to take care of themselves and make sure they get rest when they can, because when the child is awake they need to be totally on the ball.

Parents can provide 'DIY' early intervention if there is no professional support available. Start by creating some visual structure and fill the day by building positive play skills through interaction. Don't force the child to play in a traditional way, but mirror how he plays. Think of how a parent interacts with a newborn baby, copying his mannerisms and facial expressions. This is the earliest form of communication and the beginning of what autism specialists call 'intensive interaction'. For children who need constant stimulation, set up activities – cooking, washing-up, craft, camps and games.

Before a child starts school, days may seem long. Try to take the child out in the morning. It doesn't matter if it's raining – rain can mean splashing in puddles. There is no such thing as the wrong weather if you have the right clothes. Clothes can be changed when you get home. Getting the child out of the house breaks up the day, allows contact with nature and releases energy. It will also create a positive start to the day.

During your child's early years it also helps if you try to give your home the structure of a pre-school. Boredom can be a trigger. This stage can be exhausting, but it will not last forever.

> I tried to teach my child with words. They passed him by often unheard. Despairingly I turned aside 'How can I teach this child?' I cried. Into my hand he put the key, 'Come,' he said 'and play with me.' (Anon)

Early intervention can begin at home through play. Take the lead from parents like Kristine Barnett. She let her son Jake explore what he loved, engaging him by becoming part of his world. She became what these children need most of all – a trusted friend and fellow enthusiast. She focused on the 'can do's' and let a lot of the conventional 'can't' slip by until later. Jake could not tie his shoelaces, but he felt comfortable attending university lectures. Sometimes a positive learning experience is more important than ticking a box. I loved seeing Jake explaining his ideas to university students with his shoelaces untied.

Jo Worgan is another autism-mother-turned-author. She explains:

> I see autism as having many different strands. All of these strands are beautiful. They are all the colours of the rainbow intertwined intricately into the child. If you try and take away the autism by removing the strands you also take away parts of the child as they are attached to them. They are what makes them who they are. (Worgan 2012)

We do not want to remove the autism, but we do want to give the child the tools to negotiate challenges without having to retreat. We need these children to grow to become a part of society – to become inventors, artists, musicians, programmers, partners and parents. The closer we come to understanding the challenges of autism, the better we are placed to accommodate and educate without risking removing that individuality we all love.

Mirana Steffen found a very effective way to explain her son's autism.

> Say you want to watch a movie. You need a DVD player, TV and the red/white/yellow cable. If you get all of the colors put in the right place, you will see and hear your movie. If you don't get them in the right place, you may see the picture but not hear it or hear it but not see it. You may not see or hear anything, rather, get a low hum. You may see and hear everything, but with mild interference because the cords need to simply be tightened.
>
> Either way, all of the equipment for success is there. There is NOTHING missing. Someone with an ASD [autism spectrum disorder] has everything they need to be successful, but their 'cables' may not be coded 'correctly'. It's our job as parents, family members, friends, educators, and a community at large, to help our ASD buddies find their Picture, no matter what it may look like to you and me. (Steffen 2011)

Parents are instinctive and know their children best. We must listen to them. They must listen to themselves. What if Kristine Barnett had left her son with the teacher who had such low expectations and hinted that Jake was unlikely ever to read? What if Temple Grandin's mother had followed the doctor's advice and put her daughter in an institution? What if Isaac Newton had been denied a university education and forced to stay on the farm with his mother as per tradition?

Kristine's son Jake (still in his teens) has proven to be one of the greatest minds of this century and is currently lecturing at university. Temple Grandin has changed the way cattle are slaughtered all over America, has written numerous books and her amazing lectures always sell out. She's even had a Hollywood film made about her life! Isaac Newton is acknowledged as one of the greatest scientists who ever lived.

We know that children with autism like order, that they are often very visual and that they can be quite literal. They deserve beautiful resources and symbols that make sense. If a picture does not explain visually, it is pointless and the child will stop looking to the pictures for information. Knowing all these things is what made me zoom in on our visuals and realise that they needed to be perfect. The resources on the CD-ROM at the back of this book were created because symbols currently in use are not good enough for our visual learners. If a symbol does not illustrate the word, it will not help the child. It could even cause confusion. Once we realise this, the wrong symbols start to stand out. They almost shout! The child will look at the symbols and quickly assess whether they are useful or not. It is imperative that the visuals we present are spot on from the start.

Colour coding symbols from the beginning can help children with autism decode the social minefield and overcome hurdles. Colour symbols might make it easier for children with autism to learn to generalise, approach new challenges, socialise, accept behaviour rules and cope with change. Our resources and related ideas might help the child negotiate the day.

There are many autistic children who will start nursery school without a diagnosis, yet they would benefit from having autism-specific support from the start. I'd like to see all Early Years settings set up to cater for children with autism before they even arrive. With the rates of diagnosis increasing, these settings are likely to be catering for a child with autism at some point. First impressions are so important to these children. Once an opinion is formed, it tends to stick. The structures and supports we use in autism-specific settings can benefit *all* children. There is nothing harmful about displaying expectations and providing a clear visual structure for the day.

The rainbow is often used in the context of autism. It is also viewed by many as a symbol of hope. Children with autism are colourful – they are often very beautiful and, like the rainbow, they stand out. Rainbows disappear unnoticed without the right conditions. We must support these children so that they do not retreat or withdraw. They are unique, often quite brilliant, and full of possibility. We must create the right conditions to help them fulfil their potential. These conditions may be different to what we provide as standard, but they are achievable. Providing the correct levels of sunshine and rain is the only way to build a bridge and keep a rainbow in the room.

Autistic children see differently and we can cater for this. We know that when we ask them a question in the right way, we are more likely to get a favourable answer. We must also always keep a fresh eye and perfect the way we present information to them, because children with autism are seekers of the truth, and they can see infinite details. As Einstein said, 'Whoever is careless with truth in small matters can not be trusted in important affairs' (Einstein 1955). Our visuals must represent truth and decode the verbal jumble so these children can find the right direction. Once they have seen the truth, we must allow them time to process. In a world now so obsessed with speed, we teachers must step back and learn to wait. Direct these children so they know the expectation, but love them for choosing an original route. Truth, time and unconditional love will help more of our 'rainbows' reach *their* stars.

# REFERENCES

Albers, J. (1975) *Interaction of Color.* Revised Edition. New Haven, CT: Yale University Press.

Asher, J., Lamb, J., Brocklebank, D., Cazier, J., *et al.* (2009) 'A whole-genome scan and fine-mapping linkage study of auditory-visual synaesthesia reveals evidence of linkage to chromosomes 2q24, 5q33, 6p12, and 12p12.' *American Journal of Human Genetics 84,* 279–285.

Asher, J., Johnson, D., Allison, C. and Baron-Cohen, S. (2012) 'Synaesthesia and autism.' Available at www.autismresearchcentre.com/project_31_synaesth2 [accessed 27 November 2013].

Attwood, T. (2007) *The Complete Guide to Asperger's Syndrome.* London: Jessica Kingsley Publishers.

Autism Research Institute (1996) 'Interview with Temple Grandin.' Available at www.autism.com/index.php/advocacy_grandin_interview [accessed 22 October 2013].

Barnett, K. (2013a) *The Spark. A Mother's Story of Nurturing Genius.* New York: Penguin Group.

Barnett, K. (2013b) Talk About Autism. Transcript of live Q and A. Available at www.talkaboutautism.org.uk/page/liveevents/kristine_barnett.cfm [accessed 20 October 2013].

Baron-Cohen, S., Bor, D., Billington, J., Asher, J., Wheelwright, S. D. and Ashwin, C. (2007) 'Savant memory in a man with colour-form-number synaesthesia and Asperger Syndrome.' *Journal of Consciousness Studies 14,* 237–252.

Baron-Cohen, S., Johnson, D., Asher, J., Wheelwright, S., Fisher, S.E., Gregersen, P. K. and Allison, C. (2013) 'Is synaesthesia more common in autism?' *Molecular Autism 4,* 40.

BBC (2003) 'Boy's traffic light treat'. *BBC News* Wednesday, 8 January, 2003. Available at http://news.bbc.co.uk/1/hi/england/2638967.stm [accessed 12 September 2013].

Brohart, J. (2002) *The Importance Of Colors In The Life Of The Autistic Child.* Available at www.autismhelpforyou.com/role_of_colors_in_the_life_of_th.htm [accessed 20 October 2013].

Bryan, A. (1997) 'Colourful Semantics.' In S. Chiat, J. Law and J. Marshall (eds) *Language Disorders in Children and Adults: Psycholinguistic Approaches to Therapy.* London: Whurr.

Davis, S. (2008) 'Colourful Semantics – Autism.' *ITS [Integrated Treatment Services] News.* Available at www.integratedtreatments.co.uk/news/item/2/24/colourful-semantics---autism [accessed 20 October 2013].

Dunn Buron, K. and Curtis, M. (2003) *The Incredible 5-Point Scale.* Kansas: Autism Asperger Publishing Company.

Dye, M. (2011) 'Why Johnny Can't Name His Colors.' *Scientific American Mind,* May/June, 48–51.

Ebbels, S. (2007) 'Teaching grammar to school-aged children with specific language impairment using Shape Coding.' *Child Language Teaching and Therapy 23,* 67–93. Available at www.moorhouse.surrey.sch/publications-and-presentations [accessed 20 October 2013].

Einstein, A. (1955) Draft speech for Israel Independence Day.

Endow, J. (2009) *Outsmarting Explosive Behavior: A Visual System of Support and Intervention for Individuals with Autism Spectrum Disorders Autism.* Kansas: Asperger Publishing Co.

Endow, J. (2012) 'Seeing Beyond My Autism Diagnosis.' Available at http://special-ism.com/seeing-beyond-my-autism-diagnosis/#sthash.gICF9Clh.dpbs [accessed 20 October 2013].

EstherJ (2013) Discussion of synaesthesia on Wrong Planet Discussion Forum. Available at www.wrongplanet.net/postt224339.html [accessed 20 October 2013].

Evans, B.J. *et al.* (1996) *A Preliminary Study into the Aetiology of Meares-Irlen Syndrome.* London: Institute of Optometry.

Foss-Feig, J.H., Tadin, D., Schuader, K. B. and Cascio, C. J. (2013) 'A substantial and unexpected enhancement of motion perception in autism.' *Journal of Neuroscience 33,* 19, 8243–8249.

Grandin, T. (2000) 'My Experiences with Visual Thinking- Sensory Problems and Communication Difficulties.' Available at www.pbs.org/saf/1205/features/grandin2.htm [accessed 27 November 2013].

Grandin, T. (2002) *Teaching Tips For Children and Adults With Autism,* Proactive Speech Therapy. Available at http://proactivespeechtherapy.com/teaching_tips.html [accessed 20 October 2013].

Grandin, T. (2006) *Thinking in Pictures.* London: Bloomsbury Publishing.

Grandin, T. (2011) *The Way I See It: A Personal Look at Autism and Asperger's.* Second Revised Edition. Arlington, TX: Future Horizons.

Grandin, T. (2012) 'Frequently Asked Questions.' Available at http://templegrandin.com/faq.html [accessed 22 October 2013].

Gray. C. (1994) *Comic Book Conversations.* Arlington, TX: Future Horizons.

Gray. C. (2000) *The New Social Stories Book (2nd ed.).* Arlington, TX: Future Horizons.

Hammil, F. (2013) 'i had a bit of a problem today :(' Available at http://autisticandproud.wordpress.com/2013/09/10/i-had-a-bit-of-a-problem-today [accessed 27 November 2013].

Higashida, N. (2013) *The Reason I Jump: One Boy's Voice from the Silence of Autism.* Translated by K. A. Yoshida and D. Mitchell. London: Sceptre.

Irlen, H. (1998) 'Autism/Asperger Syndrome and the Irlen Method.' Available at http://irlen.com/index.php?id=70 [accessed 20 October 2013].

Irlen, H. (2010) *A Guide to Changing your Perception and Your Life. The Irlen Revolution.* Canada: Square One Publishers.

Isaacs, P. and Billet, J. (2013) *Life Through a Kaleidoscope – Memoirs of Visual Fragmentation.* Essex: Chipmunk Publishing.

Jadva, V., Hines, M. and Golombok, S. (2010) 'Infants' preferences for toys, colors, and shapes: Sex differences and similarities.' Cambridge: Centre for Family Research, Faculty of Social and Political Sciences, University of Cambridge.

Kranowitz, C. and Silver, L. (1998) *The Out-of-Sync Child: Recognizing and Coping with Sensory Integration Dysfunction.* New York: Berkley Publishing Group.

Kurtus, R. (2004) 'Synaesthesia: Hearing Colors.' Available at www.school-for-champions.com/senses/synaesthesia.htm [accessed 20 October 2013].

Lindsey, L. (2012) 'Grapheme Colour Synaesthesia Map.' Available at www.lunalindsey.com/2012/10/grapheme-color-synaesthesia-map.html [accessed 24 October 2013].

Lindsey, L. (2013) 'My Inner Life: Adventures with Aspergers.' Available at www.lunalindsey.com/2013/01/my-inner-life-adventures-with-aspergers.html [accessed 24 October 2013].

Lomber, Stephen, G., Meredith, M. Alex, Kral, A. (2010) 'Cross-modal plasticity in specific auditory cortices underlies visual compensations in the deaf.' *Nature Neuroscience 13,* 1421–1427.

Marsh, L., Pearson, A., Ropar, D. and Hamilton, A. (2013) 'Children with autism do not over imitate.' *Current Biology 23,* 7, R266–R268.

Nair, A., Treiber, J. M., Shukla, D. K., Shih, P. and Muller, R.A. (2013) *Impaired thalamocortical connectivity in autism spectrum disorder: A study of functional and anatomical connectivity.* San Diego State University's Brain Developing Imaging Laboratory

NAS (2013) 'Organising, sequencing and prioritising.' Available at www.autism.org.uk/living-with-autism/understanding-behaviour/organising-sequencing-and-prioritising.aspx [accessed 20 October 2013].

Pierce, K., Conant, D., Hazin, R., Stoner, R. and Desmond, J. (2011) *Preference for Geometric Patterns Early in Life as a Risk Factor for Autism.* Department of Neurosciences, Autism Center of Excellence, University of California. Available at www.ncbi.nlm.nih.gov/pubmed/20819977 [accessed 20 October 2013].

Pitchford, N. and Mullen, K. (2002) *How young children conceptualise colour.* McGill University, Canada, and University of Nottingham.

Steffen, M. (2011) 'Analogy for understanding autism.' Available at www.autismsupportnetwork. com/news/analogy-understanding-autism-535331 [accessed 27 November 2013].

Science Daily (2009) *Difference in the Way Children with Autism Learn New Behaviors Described.* Available at www.sciencedaily.com/releases/2009/07/090706113647.htm [accessed 20 October 2013].

Tammet, D. (2007) *Born on a Blue Day.* London: Hodder & Stoughton.

University of Western Ontario (2010) 'Research discovers super vision in deaf.' *Western News*, 11 October. Available at http://communications.uwo.ca/western_news/stories/2010/October/research_discovers_super_vision_in_deaf.html [accessed 22 October 2013].

Walker, N. and Cantello, J. (1994) *You Don't Have Words to Describe What I Experience: The Sensory Experiences of Individuals with Autism Based on First Hand Accounts.* Geneva Centre for Autism.

Williams, D. (1996) *Autism: An Inside-Out Approach: An Innovative Look at the 'Mechanics' of 'Autism' and its Developmental 'Cousins'.* London: Jessica Kingsley Publishers.

Williams, D. (1998) *Like Colour to the Blind: Soul Searching and Soul Finding.* London: Jessica Kingsley Publishers.

Worgan, J. M. (2012) *Life on the Spectrum. The Preschool Years. Getting the Help and Support You Need.* Self-published as a Kindle Edition.

# INDEX